You are promise

Martin E. Marty

Argus Communications

1974

Contents

To the members
of our summer community
on the
"Isle de Petit Detroit"

Preface

You are promise.

Those words form the name of this book
and begin both the preface
and the text itself.

They do not tell readers how to run
their lives.
The author lacks credentials
for telling anyone how to do that.

They are not designed to inspire people
or to create illusions.
Inspiration wears off in a hurry.
Illusions disappear when they are tested.

The prominence of these words suggests that the author had something special in mind. They form part of a discussion designed to cause a reader to say to himself or herself: "I never thought of it that way before." If something like that happens, some sort of change can occur, whether or not author and reader are in agreement with each other.

Before a writer dares to start such a work as this, he has to think about what he intends to accomplish, and what his qualifications may be.

My intention is to present as clearly and directly as possible an approach to living that has developed over a period of years. A way of life grows out of many experiences: of reading, thinking, getting bumped and bruised, knowing family tussles and triumphs, testing, being frustrated, speaking, and listening.

What remains after those experiences are sorted is a kind of philosophy or theology of promise. Aspects of this have shown up in my previous work, often expressed in different language and style, as in the argument of a book called *The Search for a Usable Future* or in the theme of an edited series of books on the "promise" of a number of recent thinkers. The desire also to see the development of a "core" or center in personal life is one way of expressing a durable concern.

The intentions, then, are clear. The question of credentials is more complicated. Who is qualified to impart clues about promise? Plumbers talk about plumbing, astronomers about astronomy, farmers about farming, philosophers about philosophy. As an historian, I usually talk about history. In the modern university, teachers are all trained to be specialists, to fit a groove or a slot. To speak outside one's discipline calls for daring and care.

Such narrowing customs and practices have good grounds. Who wants to listen to chatterers-in-general? But these conventions can also cause us to miss much of life and of living. The Spanish thinker who has influenced me for so long, José Ortega y Gasset, once wrote that "a man's vocation must be his vocation for a perfectly concrete, individual, and integral life, not for the social schema of a career." That translates: don't make it your calling to be concerned only with questions of your specialty, discipline, career, and the like. So far as possible, shape a life.

Caution is still in order. So we test the ideas on others, on the people we counsel or by whom we have been counseled; on friends or on people by whom we have been befriended. Some readers may be interested in the context out of which the present way of speaking has grown. A number of families to whom we are very close—I call them collegial families because we are colleagues in sharing and in trying to make sense of each other's worlds—came across a previously uninhabited island in Lake Michigan several years ago. Joined by others, we have made this a summer gathering place.

Most months of the year we are distracted metropolitanites pursuing the social schemes of our careers. But for a couple of weeks or months we gather around campfires, tents, open-air chapel pews, or summer-homes-being-built. There we enjoy Wisconsin air, read books which ordinarily would not get read, and talk about the really important things in life which do not get talked about back home. There, among other adults and young people of all ages, this plot germinated.

The other members of the community, except for our sons and foster son, were not aware of the listening and testing process that was going on. But I thank them all for the parts they have played in shaping this book and its author's ideas. I am tempted now to say to others, ''Pull up a campfire, and sit down.''

On second thought,
the concerns of this book
are not too far from the matters
which do concern an historian;
he, too, is out to discern
dread and dreams,
power and promise, in people of the past.

But the human drama
does not end with that past.

As for the future: **You are promise.**

one

Person as promise

You are promise.

Few people speak that way.
They would normally say, "You are
promising"
or "You show promise."

I mean something much different
when I say,
"You *are* promise."

A popular song of some years ago offers
a parallel. "You Are Love" says more about
a lover than a song that begins, "You are
loving" or "You are capable of loving."
"You *are* love." This tells us that, in the eyes
of the lover, the loved one embodies all that
the word love has meant through the ages.
She or he lives and breathes all that love

represents. Take the beloved away, and love will disappear from the life of the lover. Such songs overstate the case, but they help make a point about words.

If you say, "She is grace," you tell others more about a dancer or gymnast than if you say, "She is graceful" or "She has grace." If she *is* grace, she takes on all the properties of gracefulness; you will not know how grace looks or is supposed to look until you watch her in action. Similarly, the phrase, "He *is* courage" tells us that an athlete or a soldier shows all the qualities that go with heroism. These phrases are rarely used because we do not find many people who live up to them.

"You are promise." People should feel free to use this phrase more liberally. In some sense or other, it ought to apply to virtually all humans. I would say *everyone is* promise, but that might be too literal. Does someone who is "hopelessly retarded" or in a coma near death embody or represent promise? On the basis of reports of what severely handicapped and dying people have done to expand the lives of others, it might be wiser to reserve judgment. In the meantime, it seems worthwhile to use the equation sign and say that "to be human=to be promise."

Promising
is not enough

What is wrong with saying, "You are promising"? Immediately, something less comes to mind. People do not often use that phrase unless they are talking to teachers' pets or child prodigies. Sometimes parents will say it to encourage or goad a child into practicing piano or baton-twirling. "We've put so much money into your lessons and your teacher says you are promising. Now, get to work." Or the boss will use the phrase to explain why he advanced a good-looking secretary who types as if she wore mittens, while he passed over a plainer-looking, expert typist. "Miss Maurice is a promising secretary." The coach lifts up the spirit of the third-stringer: "You should come out for football again next year. You show a lot of promise."

In all of these examples, people are being used by others. The word *promising* makes sense, then, because someone is being singled out for special favor or punishment. Promise would seem to be a property that comes and goes. If the child is not useful to the parent, the secretary to the boss, or the player to the coach, the whole device of talking about promise can be discarded.

3

The word cannot be discarded, however, when one wishes to describe accurately what all people are, or how they should think of themselves. "You are promise." Promise may apply to beings and events other than yourself. Certainly, it does. And you may be many other things besides being promise. But you are nothing less than promise, and if you were less, you would be nothing. People who fail to recognize promise in themselves are not likely to live up to their potential.

You seem to be a noun

The ancients would have understood this better than we do today. They knew that a name given to a person could refer to all of his qualities. One of my favorite book titles is *I Seem To Be a Verb*. The author, Buckminster Fuller, is an intensely active man, an agent of ideas and projects; it is useful for him to think of himself figuratively as a verb. In the present context, you are a noun. Maybe you are "love." Certainly you are "promise."

In colonial New England, parents tried to sum up their hopes for a child in the name that they gave. Maybe Prudence would turn out to be prudent; Charity might become charitable; whether Chastity would remain

4

chaste was questionable. Today, parents are more likely to choose names because they sound pleasing. Promise might not sound pleasing as a name to most young women. We shall have to settle for having people think of themselves as being promise rather than bearing the name.

Humorists Roger Price and Leonard Stern in *What Not To Name the Baby* tried to develop the idea that even today people do exemplify their names. When Indians called a child Running Deer, they hoped this would influence the child to become graceful and speedy. On those terms, argue the authors, today's parents might well name a son "Cool Cat Who Makes Out Plenty," or a daughter "Goes to College" or "Walks with Wiggle."

In the Price-Stern theory, parents tend to choose names, but children are burdened with the images these names convey. Most of us, in the end, fit our names. Nicknaming can help improve a situation. How different is a Gertrude from a Trudy or a Gert, or a William from a Bill, a Billy, a Will, or a Willie! What we call ourselves or others may not have much to do with how we turn out, but how we think of ourselves does.

Unless you think about it—and these words are designed to set such thinking in motion—it is not likely that you will think of yourself as being promise. If you already do, this nudge is unnecessary, but most people think of themselves as lacking promise.

You are
projected

You are promise. Behind the word promise are the Latin words *pro* and *missio*, which together can mean "send forth," or "foretell." The word *mission* is tied up with *missio*, and that tie might rightfully scare some people away. To say that you are in the world for a mission carries with it hints of crusades and fanaticism. We think of people heading off on white chargers in every direction to combat the windmills, or of missionaries taking the next ship for a heathen land and ending up in a cannibal's boiling pot.

Pro-missio, being sent forth, can imply something more balanced, or at least more relevant than that. You were projected into a world that was not of your choosing. No one asked whether you wished to be conceived or born. But once you appeared, you had to come to terms with what it was to be in the world. Your coming makes some difference, for good or bad. "You are promise" also reminds us that you can promise trouble as well as good.

You are *pro-missio,* sent forth or projected into a world. You bring with you certain resources. The 9,200 million or more cells in your cortex represent almost limitless possibilities for being linked up with each other. Being an expert on the human brain or in mathematics was not part of my promise, so it would be dangerous for me to make too much of this point. But it would make sense that you should have at least 9,200 million to the 9,200 millionth power chances to remember or think up something. You should even stand a chance of thinking about something that had not been thought of that way before.

A world
of promise

The scientist J. B. S. Haldane once said that "the universe is not only queerer than we suppose, but queerer than we *can* suppose." Even if we multiply those 9,200 million cells to the 9,200 millionth power by the 3 billion people now alive, we still confront a universe queerer than we *can* suppose.

You are promise. You will run into unforeseen situations, "not only queerer than you suppose, but queerer than you *can* suppose." The people and contexts around you offer limitless frustrations and opportunities. To illustrate this, I take the simple example of the chessboard. *Time* magazine reports: "It has been calculated that if every man, woman, and child in the world were to spend every waking hour playing at the superhuman rate of a game a minute, it would take 217 billion years to exhaust all the variations on the first ten moves."

According to A. Cressy Morrison, if you number ten pennies in your pocket and try to draw them out blind in sequence, putting each coin back in your pocket after each draw, the chances of drawing 1 is 1 in 10, of drawing 1 and 2 in succession is 1 in 100, on up to the chances of drawing 1 to 10 in succession, for which the odds are 1 in 10 billion.

To see no promise in minds or moves, then, is to deny the unforeseeably queer nature of the universe. To see these odds and options makes it difficult for anyone to say, "Everything has been tried" or "It's fate." People who easily surmount that difficulty, however, still fail to see promise. Getting them to change is a full-time activity of the people we call catalysts, charismatics, therapists, or friends. A catalytic person changes others as if by sudden chemistry. A charismatic seems to have special gifts of leadership. A therapist heals professionally. A friend takes time to talk with someone else and helps the other person think together with him. All four types assume that people who have not thought of themselves as being promise can begin to do so, and that such thinking will make a difference.

Now
for the opposite

A second word game is in order. What do we call the opposite of promise? To coin a new word might be clever or cute, but I prefer to work with what is at hand. In this case, the word is hardly at hand. In fact, I had to go to the twelve-volume *Oxford English Dictionary* to find it in faint print.

"Promiseless, a. *rare.* Devoid of promise."* The word is illustrated in the dictionary by a line from a poem written in 1882, "The promiseless calm of the present was dull with the dusk of night."

Promiseless is a rare word, but it does exist, even if only in the Oxford dictionary. Sometimes a coined word or a rare word will help us think more deeply about a matter than will an overworked one. The language will not necessarily be richer if we run around saying "promiseless," but we can do our own thinking on the basis of it, before burying it back in the rare words section of a gigantic dictionary.

You are promiseless. That would mean

you are without potential, resource, or worth. Your ideas would not matter, your being could be ignored. You are a hopeless case. The Greek philosopher Heraclitus said, "If you do not expect it, you will not find the unexpected, for it is hard and difficult to find." And you, as promiseless, do not expect the unexpected. Heraclitus also said, "He who does not hope for the unexpected will not find it." And you do not hope to find it.

If you *are* promiselessness, nothing ever works right. The Jewish schlemiel "falls on his back and breaks his nose," and he has found company in you. But we will take you seriously and not make a joke of it. Many people have good reason to think they are promiseless because they have not experienced fulfillment of promises. The poet W. H. Auden really saw what many overlook in juvenile delinquents when he observed that they had "never heard of any world where promises were kept, or one could weep because another wept."

The way the world regards and reacts to them, you would think that the poor, the ghetto dwellers, the handicapped and ill and aged, all prisoners and delinquents are not promise. Yet they are in the clear majority among the human beings in our queer and unexpected universe. Mentioning them (you?) here serves to remind us that promise is not always visible and expected. But we must learn to expect the unexpected, to hope for it. Only then can it be recognized. And this reminds us that promise need not always look like genius or come from advantage.

Of worms
and wolves

If you are promise, then you *are* "that which affords a strong or reasonable ground of expectation of something to come, especially of future good; a pledge, earnest, forerunner, preindicator; something that leads one confidently to expect (good) results." The *Oxford English Dictionary,* which we shall now ceremoniously close and shelve, adds that all this is *"fig.,"* a figurative use of the word promise. We are talking figures, images, signs, and symbols.

Such images have great weight in determining how we think and act. Negatively, suppose you are convinced that the humble thing to do is to think of yourself as nothing. One figure that is sometimes used for this is, "I am a worm and no man." This phrase is found in the Bible, so we are not predisposed to say that it has nothing to do with what the human person is. But if it represents the self-image of a person who offers himself to others, trouble lies ahead. Who wants to be loved by a worm? Humans want to be loved by other humans of promise.

The French artist Georges Rouault once did a series of prints on the theme "Man is a wolf to man." Man is, or at least he can be, a wolf. Unfortunately for the wolf, he has acquired the not-quite-accurate image of being, well, wolfish—greedy, savage, a predator. Unfortunately for the human race, some men and women have been wolfish.

We do not know whether somewhere early in his career Attila the Hun was reached by someone who gave him a negative self-image. "Attila, you are a wolf to man." So he acted greedily or savagely. Maybe no one had to provide Nero or Caligula with nasty symbols of themselves. Hitler may have been a wolf to man without having someone provide the label; the same may be true of Al Capone. In fact, some of history's dastards certainly convinced themselves that they were serving noble purposes. But studies of assassins and mass murderers in our time show that, in many instances, people who once should have been important to them crippled them

12

somehow by offering them self-images that led to disaster for others. "I am a worm and act the worm part; I am a wolf and act wolfishly."

Foolish
promise

On the other hand, one may act on the basis of more promising images or figures. When we take this turn, it is important to remember that positive self-images cannot work miracles. Or, rather, they *can* work miracles: they may make fools out of ordinarily decent people. Back in the 1920s, the United States was visited by a persuasive Frenchman, Émile Coué. He imparted the formula, "Every day, and in every way, I am becoming better and better."

Encyclopaedia Britannica summarized his view of change. "Based on the power of imagination rather than that of the will, his naïve system utilized formulas, repeated again and again in a confident voice, especially at a time when the mind was most receptive, to sink into the subconscious and to eliminate ideas tending to cause distress and disease." Now, if you go around repeating again and again in a confident voice, "I am promise," let us hope that some friend will tap you on the shoulder and tell you that you have been reading the wrong books, or rather, reading the right books in the wrong way.

The suggestion that you are promise does not imply that all will turn out well for you if only you think positively. Cults of positive thinkers abound. They can help correct some human faults. But they also can help people create illusions or fail to come to terms with themselves. The doctor who has the courage to cut the guff and finally tell someone who complains of an inferiority complex, "You are inferior," does the human race a favor. We can also surmise that the doctor then goes on to offer hope as well as guidance in self-appraisal, healing after he has cleared the air.

**Problems
with promise**

The fact that you *are* promise, that you afford "a strong or reasonable ground of expectation of something to come, especially of future good," does not solve anything. It will not unlock the mysteries of this queer universe. It will not offer many answers, though we can hope that it will lead to better questions and clearer problems. Being promise does not mean that the tragic will be removed. People die. You

14

will. Worlds end. Ours will. ("Did you say in 2 billion years or 2 million years?" asked the woman of the lecturing scientist. "I said about 2 billion years." "Whew!" She wiped her brow. "For a minute I thought you had said 2 million.") The changes that matter are not those borne of evasions.

You are promise. Living that concept can cause trouble. The promiseless have ways of hiding in the woodwork or against the wallpaper. Those who drift through days aimlessly as does the leaf fallen on an almost idle pool can go virtually unnoticed in their decay. The athletic coach takes the player of promise and puts him in the front line. The scrimmage is bruising, and any sensible champion must now and then utter some black and blue curses to match his bruises. He shows promise, so someone invests in him, at considerable expense to his comfort.

The future
changes the present

To say that you are promise is to notice that while you can either cope with or savor the present, you are a sign of the future. In some senses, you live there already. The young person who is assured an inheritance at age twenty-one may act differently than he would if he did not know it. The knowledge may be "for better or for worse." Some people, sprung free of necessity by such knowledge, make use of their time by preparing for the day they will realize this promise. If they have a touch of grace, their preparation will be almost invisible and the future wealth will never be mentioned to those near them. If not, they may turn playboy, knowing they can always be bailed out of trouble by the potential of future wealth. The point is that promise can alter self-images.

Consider the athlete who has the promise of becoming a champion and believes it. The tennis player will be more willing to practice that serve a few more thousand times than if she thinks of herself as a born loser. The track star will run the extra miles even though his lungs are bursting, or the skater will skate once more around the rink even if his toes feel as if they are being guillotined. Those who have told themselves they stand no chance of finishing the race rarely finish.

Someone has said that the great thinker is the one who knows already what others do not know as yet. His or her thoughts somehow focus on a future promise that lies out of range for those who do not engage in daring thinking. An army that knows the decisive battles have already been fought can engage in mopping-up battles with a different attitude than would a hopeless, promiseless military force entering just one more contest.

The self-image or figure even changes one's appearance and manners. The beautiful girl welcomes a new gown, not only because she is beautiful but because it helps her to become beautiful. The transformation of the ugly duckling who is freed or required by circumstances to live into the beauty of that gown has also made up the plot of many a film or fairy tale. In the extreme, such outcomes belong only in fairy tales; there is only so much we can do about our appearance. But the new gown promises glamor and excitement and is linked in the girl's mind with bright occasions. Being associated with it, wearing it, readies her for glamor and excitement.

We are back to the need for reinforcement from the playful Price-Stern theory of names and images. For example, they say, "Odd and far-out names, like Quandra, Elmarie, Imelda, Haralda, Fleur, Zenobia, etc., indicate the girl will be some sort of odd or far-out type. She'll . . . certainly wear leotards around the house and own a lot of black clothes." She lives into her image. But *"Rebecca* is beautiful." (Please be, Rebecca, for Price-Stern's sakes and

Promise can alter self-image.

my sake!) About someone called Sis it will be said, "*Sis* has to take care of her Mother, so she becomes an art teacher in grade school."

Being "promising" can be as nauseating
as being the teacher's pet
or mamma's boy or girl genius.
Being promise means that you recognize
the open future
and look for the unexpected.

Such recognizing and looking
comes easily to only a few.

We may assume that all of the people
some of the time
and some of the people all of the time
have the problem of promiselessness.
The word is rare,
but the state of mind is not.

We will take a close look.

two Threats to meaning

You are promiselessness.

It would be inaccurate
to apply the word *promiseless*
to many, or perhaps
to any, human beings.

But the fact remains that most of us
feel devoid of promise or future
often enough
that we have to recognize it as a problem.

You can translate promiseless in many
ways. Before this diagnosis is over, we shall
see that most frequently it translates into
meaningless, futile, plotless, or boring. Diagnosis may be a rather heavy word. It
might suggest that we are going to put on a
white gown and stethoscope and have you
speak up—figuratively, of course—from a
sprawl on a couch. Some people are carried by promiselessness to such a point that
they do need medical and psychiatric aid.
(Going to the doctor can itself be a sign that
you are promise.) Here we shall restrict

ourselves to the humbler task of observing and reporting how the feeling of being devoid of promise affects people in ordinary circumstances.

One way to do this is to follow a person through the hours of the day or times of the week and year. How does meaninglessness or futility, plotlessness or boredom rob people of a sense of promise in the ordinary course of events?

The day
without prospect

Morning. I should steal a habit from the dictionary and write *"fig."* after the word because in the following, four times of the day are used figuratively. The absence of promise that we associate with morning can come at any time of day in any day of our lives. But the symbolism will become clear in the telling, and there are literal reasons for linking the feeling with the time of day.

Morning inspires the nothing-to-look-forward-to sense in those who do not feel or know promise. Different personality types do greet morning in different ways, and it is said that different bodily systems respond differently to sunup. These differences may have little to do with what any of us actually thinks about the universe when we are truly awake. And we do not get to pick the biological pace and manner of our awakenings.

Albert Schweitzer once admitted that he could not bound forth to face a new day with a song in his heart. He, as a physician in Africa and as a student of world history, knew too much about suffering to be anything but grave as he took on some of the burdens of the day. Maybe Mme. Schweitzer was a bounder-forther; she had to live with grave old Albert, so a song might have helped carry her through—and it might have given him the painful sense of a delightful alternative for greeting the day. In any case, we do not fault Schweitzer because morning represented a literal problem for him. Figuratively, it was promise. His response to gravity shows us that he knew that.

Even those who have less difficulty arising than others—and I did not imply it was *fun* for Mme. Schweitzer, or for those who can jump up baritoning "Oh! What a beautiful morning; Oh! What a beautiful day"— probably have days when the whole weight of promiselessness greets them at that hour. Empathy with the graver risers is not hard to express.

So it is morning. The alarm rings. It is even *Monday* morning. A whole week lies

Morning inspires the
nothing-to-look-forward-to sense
in those who do not feel
or know promise ...

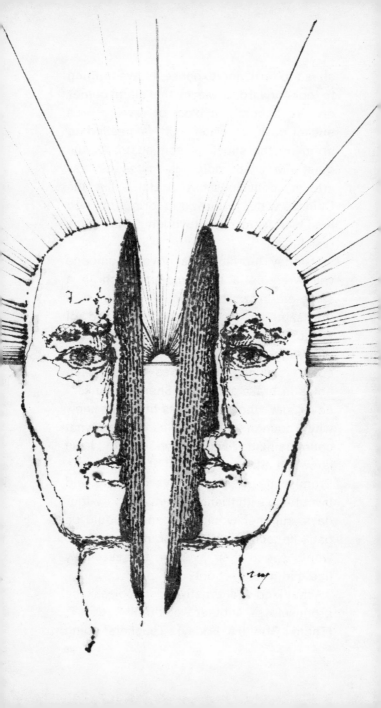

ahead in terrifying expanse. I have nothing to look forward to. Maybe that alarm comes on like a bomb, a blast of reveille or a bucket-dash of water that is needed to bring on the shock of coming to. Or the quiet FM clock-radio insinuates its way into my consciousness. It still is like the Chinese water torture: drip, drip, drip. I go mad with its incessant working away at my resistance.

Monday morning. Hangover. Someone will wrap up a same-old-sandwich in a same-old-brown-bag, and I will head off to the same-old-factory. Near the end of World War II, when I was able-bodied but underage for the draft, I spent a summer countersinking both sides of eighteen holes in brake shoes for Sherman tanks. I never saw where the shoes fit, never knew why I countersank the holes or even what countersinking was. I would not have known a Sherman tank if it had hit me. Promise meant that the day would end, and I would be with friends again. In eighty-four days, summer would end and I would be back in school. What about those who would spend their lives on the assembly line and not in school?

What kind of alternative is school, ask the promiseless? Another week until T. G. I. F. (Thank God It's Friday). Teachers going through boring routines, administrators keeping tabs on me, bells chopping up the day into meaningless and tedious fragments, everyone preparing me to get into lockstep for that assembly line or office. Not that this is the attitude of everyone who goes to school, or even most of them. But those who are becoming part of the narcotic culture will tell you that the boring, nothing-to-look-forward-to mood is what led them to try to escape through drugs. And most people will admit that the Monday morning mood hits them now and then.

The office offers little more. I am a salesman and must compete. So they gave me an award for selling more paper clips or clothespins than someone else; is the world better or changed for the effort? I have stared at all those barren walls of motel rooms from coast to coast, or at least throughout my territory. For what? To look forward to another year of staring at motel walls, flirting with bored waitresses, listening to dreary pep talks made by robots who do not believe what they are saying? Or, the typist might say, "I improved my typing speed and the boss complimented me. Did he notice my improvement or did he just want a date? Do I have to fight him off, just like the last boss? To what purpose?"

Yet morning is supposed to represent

promise. "Daybreak, another new day. . . ."
Popular songs, folk songs, serious poetry all conspire to create that idea. It is an empty promise. I have *cause* to have nothing to look forward to.

Sometimes promiselessness is based on past defeat: Yesterday I had resolved to make a difference in the world, but failure came. In a vague way, I feel guilty. The priest or pastor says, "You are forgiven," and I don't feel a thing. My psychiatrist wants to know why, after all these years and all this time, I keep on feeling guilty. Guilt may run much, much deeper than this, but in a way guilt is meaty and tangible. I can get a hold on it and define it or deal with it. When I do not feel guilty but still have no sense of meaning, it is a worse problem.

Sleep was a kind of nirvana, a suspension of purpose or promise and their alternatives. A pleasant figure for dying. I would roll over and turn back to it, but the alarm rings again. I have no choice but to get up. The treadmill. The rat race. Clichés, by now, but I have no better words. Back to the salt mines. Will I make any difference to any other human? I do not expect the unexpected because each day is like every other.

If there is to be meaning, it is up to me, they say. I must be a "stalker of meaning," says Jean-Paul Sartre. Life has no meaning by nature and in advance: "It is up to you to give it a meaning, and value is nothing else than this meaning which you choose." But how can I bring meaning to life, when it is precisely meaning that I lack? If I *had* meaning, I could bring it to the day and all would be well. But the circle of meaninglessness is not easily interrupted. I am not naturally promise.

Springtime
and childhood

People use other figures to signal promise. Springtime is one. Spring is the time of awakening, of planting, of budding, the season for juices to flow. For a moment, its beauty lifts the soul, but before long I turn thoughtful and see springtime in the cycle of the years. Income tax comes due, report cards bring their quiet, drab doom, and I plant merely to repeat what has gone before.

Maybe I will not even see the fruit of any of these efforts. Where, then, is the promise? In the year of Oregon's centennial, a light-hearted brewery sent out, as a public relations gesture, an Oregon Do-It-Yourself Kit. In a plastic bag, strapped to a wooden tongue depressor, was a tiny pine seedling. Find the right place and plant it. It represents promise. If all goes well, in 15 years you can hang Christmas tree ornaments on it if you are careful, because it does strain under the weight. In 50 years or so, you can place your chair under it and enjoy some shade, and in 80 years you can use it to tie up one end of a hammock, providing a neighbor was provident enough to plant another Oregon Do-It-Yourself Kit. And in 200 years the tree will be full-grown. "You deserve a plaque."

So it is with much that is called promise in life. By the time the promiser or reminder finishes talking we find that the fruits and benefits are so remote and so farfetched that, while we may deserve a plaque, there is no sense of achievement. The days of the 200 years we must wait are still like each other, having little to offer. The odds on my tree getting trampled are good. Meanwhile, dogs find it a convenient stopping place for indignities performed in the course of their pursuits.

A third image of promise in new beginnings is the child. Childhood represents promise: any child, we were told, could grow up to be president. Of course, there are some limits to one's achievement. A boy might not become a football star if he were destined to reach only 130 pounds. His sister stood little chance of becoming an opera star if she came equipped with a

Spring is the time of awakening,
of planting, of budding,
the season for juices to flow.

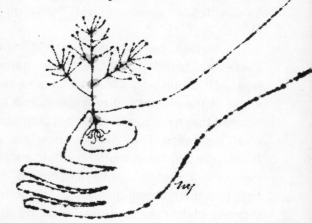

squeaky voice. And that White House prospect was dimmed not only by limitations in one's basic equipment, but also by who and where you were. Women, blacks, and many others need never apply. Still, you knew what people meant.

Childhood is gone now, however. Once, according to the folklore, the boy entertained himself with the promise of becoming a cowboy or a fireman; later, it would be a jet pilot. Now he is a shoe salesman or a computer programmer. His marriage is sufficiently dreary that he cannot look for more prospect there. The dreams have died, and nothing big lies ahead. The protection of mother or nurse is gone. The poet Rainer Maria Rilke speaks for mother and child, "Where, oh, where, are the years when you simply displaced for him, with your slender figure, the surging abyss?"

The mother "hid so much from him then; made the nightly-suspected room harmless." She nurtured his dreams and fed some of the illusions. But he grew, and he learned that his parents could not take care of all his needs. They did not know everything, could not do everything, could not be everywhere. Father is weak, and flawed. He lies. And the children grow up to forget the promise of the dreams. The adult drops into church for Christmas Eve and hears the innocence and promise of childhood extolled once again. He is no longer touched. After a moment's pause, he goes out into the night.

The styles
of boredom

Noon. If mornings stand for the kind of futility that is linked with the sense that there is nothing to look forward to, through the ages noon (*fig.*) signals many kinds of boredom. Philosophers and psychologists never tire of trying to diagnose it. They have not come near reaching its depths. Maybe those depths are lost in mystery.

You have felt this boredom. "I can't quite put my finger on what is wrong." One or two film makers—Antonioni in Italy comes to mind—have successfully depicted it. This noonday torpor of the soul is visible on the faces of the drifting, lost people. They go to parties without enthusiasm, make love without ecstasy, spend money and consume goods without enjoyment.

You are promiselessness. So it is when the noonday demon reaches you. Yes, *demon*. Back when people found it easy to account for what went wrong by looking around the spirit world, they decided that devils were responsible. One devil was the

33

daemon meridianus, the demon of the meridian or noontime. Our forefathers' explanation was not much worse than most of ours.

At noon, there is no sense of drama. Everything slows and stills in the stretch of the day. Maybe there is sun, but at meridian there are no shadows to provide contrast. When climate dictates, sensible people adjust their bodies to what their souls know. It is time for siesta. Better not to think. Flies buzz just enough to let the sleeper know that the universe has not ground to a stop; the napper stirs to chase the fly but welcomes return to the nothing of the sweaty nap.

Perhaps it is a rainy Sunday noon. The newspapers provide diversion for late risers in the form of padded-out comics and features. The coffee is cold, and the orange peels shrivel, their pleasant odor having turned rancid in the mix of stale cigarette smoke. The children have stirred themselves to Sunday School down the block and returned home. "What shall we do?" It is catching: When I was a child, I was told by adults—accidentally, I hope—that heaven meant endless rest and repose. It sounded much like those spacious Sunday afternoons. Everlasting. Hell, of course, was out of the question. If only we had been

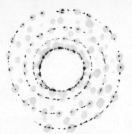

At noon, there is no
sense of drama.
Everything slows and stills
in the stretch of the day.

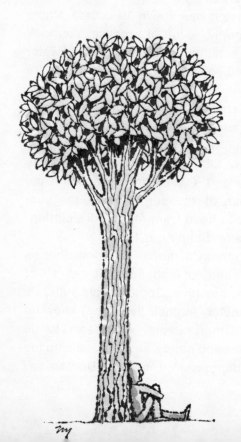

told of purgatory, where *something* happened. There change occurred, and drama was possible.

On the surface, the noonday demon produces something like anxiety. But save anxiety for three o'clock in the morning. *That* kind of anxiety grows from the sense that time presses in on us. We do not have enough time to live, to be. At noon, time is too much with us. The seconds drag as melancholy sets in.

The case is overdrawn, of course. Noon, taken literally, is full of promise. You look out on a summer's day and see water skiers, and you take to the beach. These are the best hours. Or the morning chill is gone, and you can take a walk. The late risers or late starters have finally wiped the sleep from their eyes, and noon is their most productive time. Those who do not like the shadows and the darkness welcome the brightness of the sun. Not all the sunbathers are fresh from Antonioni's cutting-room floors. Sunning is fun.

The noonday demon of boredom, then, is not confined to high noon. It can afflict people at any time. Some people suffer its effects acutely all their lives. They know no escape. Other people, who seem to be productive and happy, suddenly fall into the kind of depression it inspires. Doctors say that depression is sometimes a physiological problem, and that certain drugs can alleviate it.

Amateurs prescribe drugs for themselves to combat boredom. Some students on drugs blame their teachers for the boredom that led them to drugs for kicks or escape. Others are honest enough to recognize that their teachers are not boring, that nothing special is wrong with the outside world. In our own souls—there is where the void is. Outside it may be noon, but within me it may be night. George Bernanos's "little priest," in *The Diary of a Country Priest,* sees his values and beliefs quietly die. "God! I breathe, I inhale the night, the night is entering into me by some inconceivable, unimaginable gap in my soul. I, myself, am the night."

A deadly
sin?

In the Middle Ages, not knowing what else to do with this torpor, the clerics did what they were expert at doing. They called it a sin. In fact, it was a deadly sin, a capital sin. It stood at the head of a column of sins, and others grew out of it. The deadly sin of sloth comes off badly in modern translation. We usually think of sloth as mere laziness, the desire to linger too long in the bath or to postpone homework. Why should laziness be a deadly sin?

Sloth, however, implied much more than being a bit relaxed or dragged out. In medieval times, people called it *accedie* or *acedia.* The word dropped out of the dictionary for centuries, and for some time experts alone used it in conversations with their peers.

Now, acedia is working its way back into English dictionaries because we need the word. Our affluent culture produces consumers. They earn and consume but experience little pleasure. They have acedia. Insulated from death and disease—Grandmother is in a nursing home far away, and Grandfather was done up by cosmetologists before you saw him amid the dyed flowers at the mortuary—the child grows up without facing the horror around him. It has moved within him. A welfare society offers him social security, but he is not satisfied. Causes bid for his attention. The crusade of the week would like to sign him up. Propagandists word him nearly to death. Defensively, having heard all the sermons, he wears the lapel button: "I am neither for nor against apathy."

The futility of the days that haunts the inhabitants of skid row is understandable. What if all days of many people were dull noon? The sin of sloth was a not-caring state. That is what acedia literally meant.

Paul Elmen calls acedia involuntary apathy—the sense of being seized by nothing. All activities are equally meaningless. Fear of death leads us to think we will be snatched away too soon from meaning. Acedia is the fear that not even death will snatch us away from the nothing. It is a secret loneliness, "aversion to openness," sadness in the face of the good.

We may feel that these medieval sins no longer apply for us. We are neither saints nor spiritual geniuses, and the language of soul is a bit embarrassing. Why take so seriously the tired meowings of a suburban kid sulking in the locker room? Why give big and formal names to little selfishnesses? This kind of boredom is a luxury that only well-off people in rich societies can afford. Peasants and others who are neither pitied nor self-pitying are granted no such luxury.

The therapy, in these cases, goes something like this. Tell people to pep up. Take a cool shower to get the blood flowing. Have the kids run around the block. Tell them to start something and the rest will follow. Take away the name for the disease and the disease will lapse back into anonymity. Such advice might be a good cold-water bath for those who try to draw attention to themselves. It might separate those with acute problems from those who are going through passing boredom. But try to tell our artists and psychologists, our reporters and counselors that this void feeling is rare and they will not take you seriously. The demon will not lightly be chased off into the desert with Saint Anthony, out where temptations are especially ferocious.

Summer would serve as another figure to match noon. The dog days come. Stagnation sets in. The crops are coming to maturity, ripening without our involvement or work. Strange as it may sound, youth is a like image. While youth seems full of promise to everyone else, much of what we see as adolescent crisis has to do with the absence of promise associated with nameless, faceless boredom. Everyday expectations are lowered, not raised. The young person learns that not everything is going to turn out right. Something in him atrophies. He does not know how to recognize or enjoy the good when it comes.

**Fear
and evasion**
Evening. As in Saturday evening or New Year's Eve. You are promiselessness, meaninglessness, or futility if all of life is

symbolized by the frantic sense seen among the desperate on festive occasions.

What follows is not an attack on parties or orgies. Just as the noontime siesta in itself was not the problem, so the seasonal fiesta can be part of the legitimate rhythm of life.

The fiestas or carnivals celebrated by some societies in certain seasons provide opportunities for letting off steam. That is healthy. Celebrations make room for gaiety and for relief from ordinary, everyday boredom. People are probably better off for it. A certain spontaneity and grace marks the occasions. Similarly, many people in our society know what to do with Saturday evening and New Year's Eve.

I chose these times as images because they represent some of the moments when the hollowness in our culture most shows. People of promise can use festive occasions as times for expressing otherwise buried aspects of their personalities. The haunted people, however, need an excess of noise and activity to forget.

Playwright Tennessee Williams prefaced *The Rose Tattoo* with this appropriate comment:

Whether or not we admit it to ourselves, we are all haunted by a truly awful sense of impermanence. I have always had a particularly

You are promiselessness, meaninglessness
or futility of all of life

is symbolized by the frantic sense
seen among the desperate
on festive occasions.

keen sense of this at New York cocktail parties, and perhaps that is why I drink the martinis almost as fast as I can snatch them from the tray. . . . The moment after the phone has been hung up, the hand reaches for a scratch pad and scrawls the notation: "Funeral at five, Church of the Holy Redeemer, don't forget flowers." And the same hand is only a little shakier than usual as it reaches, some minutes later, for a highball glass that will pour a stupefaction over the kindled nerves. Fear and evasion are the two little beasts that chase each other's tails in the revolving wire cage of our nervous world. They distract us from feeling too much about things. Time rushes toward us with its hospital tray of infinitely varied narcotics, even while it is preparing us for its inevitably fatal operation.*

Impermanence, fear and evasion mark the adult, cocktail-party world. Young people who have found their way out through hard drugs report that this way out is not fun at all. R. H. Berg tells us, "Contrary to claims of indescribable delights by some drug takers, most people abuse drugs to relieve anxiety. They're not pursuing pleasure, they just hurt less on drugs. This is true also of hard-narcotic users. A heroin addict told a reporter, 'You don't even know what I'm talking about; you feel okay all the

*Tennessee Williams, *The Rose Tattoo* (New York: New Directions, 1951), pp. viii, x.

time. Me, it costs me $100.00 a day just to stop hurting so much.'"

In the United States in 1969, 90 million new prescriptions were issued for mild tranquilizers; antidepressive drugs appeared in 17 million new prescriptions; 12 million people reported using pot at least once. Those figures have since climbed. Add to these the unreported use of drugs, stimulants, aspirins, sleeping pills, and the like. "Fear and evasion are the two little beasts that chase each other's tails."

Saturday night is the time for stupefaction, for noise, for the beer bust, or the joy ride. Frank Sinatra once gave two prescriptions for the aftermath. He did not care how people get through the night. Some use Scotch and some use religion—anything, just so they get through the night. In this symbolism, sex without purpose or pleasure has its place in the world of consumers and users-of-others. To the casual observer the Beautiful People are having a good time. *Some* of them *may* be. Envy them.

Autumn
and the autumn of life
Our little survey of the hours and their corresponding seasons brings us to autumn, the parallel to evening. Autumn

has its beauty, as does Saturday night. But the beauty is tinged with the sense of impermanence, and the sweetness in the air is the result of the decaying of leaves lying in the gutters and valleys. In Munich, the Germans know what to do with autumn, and the rest of the world is following. *Oktoberfest* is a beer orgy at which adultery is not a crime, silence is forbidden, and gluttony is admired. The citizens and the tourists forget; they enjoy the harvest past and the fresh brew. They forget and let fear and evasion chase each other's tails. Tomorrow?

In the cycle of life, we have reached the promiselessness of maturity. More doors have closed; more promises have been forgotten, and fewer new ones are to be made.

The telltale traces of autumnal decay are pushed aside or covered up as adults try to regain lost youth. Dignified professors still safely this side of senility do what they can to try to be "kids," to adopt youthful styles and sensibilities. Suburban mothers serve as cheerleaders for their sixth-graders: "Get in there and go steady." They identify with their dating daughters. Report cards are earnestly compared at bridge clubs, while parents relive their disappearing youth. "Naked in middle age," complained one mother about herself as she saw that young people still had each other. They were mobile and free to form communes and have community. They found ways to keep defenses up, to insulate themselves against reality. She was defenseless, alone, naked.

In maturity, you are caught between, just as evening is a between time and autumn is a between season. Sam Levenson, the humorist, speaks up for the cheated: "When I was a boy, my father was the boss. Now I'm a man, my son is the boss. When does it get to be my turn?" Being boss is no special fun, either.

If evening is in-between-time with its mixed signals—making some people happy but many fearful and evasive—the middle of the night leaves little confusion or doubt about terror.

At three o'clock
in the morning

3 A.M. We have set our clock figuratively. Admittedly, any time in the middle of the night will do. Perhaps you sleep through every night of the year; many do. But for those who cannot, the "3 A.M. awareness" is common. As novelist F. Scott Fitzgerald put it, "In a real dark night of the soul it is always three o'clock in the morning, day after day." Others experience it upon

In a real dark night of the soul
it is always three o'clock
in the morning,
day after day.

awakening from a daytime nap. Maybe it arrives unheralded when you are wide awake and about some other business.

Earlier we were making a distinction between plain old boredom and apparently uncaused acute boredom. Now we must draw a line between ordinary anxiety and anxiety that does not wait for occasions, even if it makes its most regular appearance at three in the morning. For the special case of boredom or acedia, the definition came from the Middle Ages. In the matter of anxiety, a contemporary put it best, even if he used a long word that says little to most people. Paul Tillich spoke of "ontological anxiety."

Forget about the word. We can try to understand about the condition or state to which it refers. A human being suddenly becomes aware of the threat of nonbeing. Why is there something, and not nothing? Why do I exist, instead of not existing? Instantly, the precariousness of existing begins to come clear; maybe existence is a dream, a nightmare, an illusion. In any case, meaninglessness is haunting, and I experience "anxiety of meaninglessness." This is caused or aroused "by the loss of a spiritual center, of an answer" in any form "to the question of the meaning of existence."

Fear is related to definite objects. You are afraid of that brute on the opponent's football team. You have to face him in this afternoon's game. There is something you can do about the anxiety borne of that fear. You can isolate it and give it a name. That in itself is helpful; you do not fear other things because you concentrate on fearing The Brute. Or you can chicken out and quit the team or fake an injury. More typically, you will go to the locker room and throw up a few times and then get out there and play like mad.

You are anxious about performing. You know you will be all fingers when you reach for the guitar in front of a crowd. You are sure that when you open your mouth, nothing will come out. Your palate is dry and fuzzy, and you break out in a cold sweat. You can define that fear and do something about it. Even at 3 A.M. you may have normal anxiety if you are to undergo surgery tomorrow. None of these fears signals the cutting off of promise. Facing and possibly conquering any one of them is part of your becoming a football star, a good member of a musical group or a healthy person.

But unoccasioned anxiety that sneaks up on you resists definition and suggests no simple response. You know one thing: It reminds you of the end of all promise. You are finite. The couple of cubic feet you now occupy will one day not be occupied by you, and the atoms that now constitute you will have been dispersed. The time of your being will have moved on. Normal anxiety is based on what comes at you from without; basic anxiety comes from within. You are threatened with destruction by nothingness, with nonbeing.

Not too much should be made of this anxiety. I doubt if everyone faces it regularly and deeply. Some people confuse it with neurotic anxiety, which is a psychosocial matter. More people link it with fear, which we have seen has different causes. No doubt many people, when they hear it described, consider it the fad or the luxury of bored intellectuals. Not too many young people experience it, in part because the possibility of death and nonbeing is not yet as vivid for them as it is for older people.

Still, having awakened at 3 A.M., you do wonder what promise might mean for you in your short time and small space. You light a cigarette, turn the radio on, try to think and not to think, to read and not to read. A trip to the bathroom, a blink at the bright lights—these do little to help change matters. You know in your bones that you matter little in the eternal mess. "I am no big deal, and before long I will be no deal at all." You purge the thought, but it comes back.

Winter
in the heart

The winter of the soul's discontent expresses itself. The landscape is barren, nothing is productive, the chill is deep and may be lethal. In our comparisons to the span of life, this is old age. Not all old people are more anxious about nonbeing than younger people are. Many, as we well know, face futures with more sense of promise than do some of their juniors. But there are special occasions in the sleeplessness of age when this 3 A.M. feeling or awareness presses most vividly. The suicide note from an aged person expresses well what we have meant by promiselessness: "So tired of buttoning and unbuttoning."

While the hand of death cannot be permanently stayed, morning comes to those who live, and spring follows winter. A person experiencing profound anxiety does not have to wallow in it and become paralyzed. For Paul Tillich, there is "the courage to be." Courage affirms the present moment and the space one now holds; one can begin by being courageous. Courage recognizes that I am dependent on others and other things for life, and I learn to accept this attachment. Courage accepts the threat that what I have and know may be lost.

Be courageous. If only it were that easy, the 3 A.M. shock could be overcome. The approach to it is more complex, however. We have to learn more about ourselves and our promise, about help from other persons and events, before the pep talk about having courage makes sense.

You are promise.

You will find this is true
to the degree that your life
takes on meaning.

No answers are assured beginners
in the quest,

but the venture with good questions
is worth the effort.

Better the search
than the torpor of siesta
or the evasion of fiesta;

You are promise
to the degree
that your life
takes on meaning.

better the seeking
than the apathy of depressed mornings
or the shock of anxiety
in the middle of the night.

Such is the testimony of those
who have learned to have the courage
to accept the promise that is their lives.

three Beginnings of fulfillment

The poet Walt Whitman
did not think much of the way humans
faced their meaninglessness.
At any rate, he admired the animals.

"They do not sweat and whine
about their condition.
They do not lie awake in the dark
and weep for their sins,
They do not make me sick
discussing their duty to God."

Humans have little choice
but to face up to their condition.

Not everyone is as acutely aware of the
problem of promise as are those described
in the previous chapter. Many can bound
up to face the day, be productive at noon,

enjoy a healthy party come evening, and sleep through the night. Spring represents possibility, summer provides vacation, autumn evokes poetic beauty, and winter offers a good rest. Childhood is promise, youth offers experiment, maturity displays fulfillments, and age is rich in peace. Those who greet life on such terms probably feel that there was too much melodrama in the last chapter's description. We played into the hands of those who sweat and whine, who lie awake and weep.

Assume that most people live between the extremes. They cannot avoid thought about the meaning of existence. Huston Smith took a sentence from the French thinker Merleau-Ponty and wrote a whole book on it. "Because we are present to a world, we are condemned to meaning." Animals are not "present" to a world. They take what the hour gives, eating as they can and must. Humans have to make sense of a world of impressions. They are, thereby, "condemned to meaning."

Some modern thinkers, even some religious scholars who are supposed to be in the "meaning" and "meanings" business, believed that the search would mean less to people in the future than in the past. Out of the sight of death and protected by a social welfare state, they could live happy and healthy lives. True, a few intellectuals, neurotics, and artists might find it fashionable to ask bigger questions. But for most people they would pass from the scene. Their prediction has not generally come to be true.

Albert Camus, novelist and philosopher, once said, "Judging whether life is or is not worth living amounts to answering the fundamental question of philosophy. . . . I therefore conclude that the meaning of life is the most urgent of questions." Before Camus the American John Dewey had written, "Meaning is . . . more precious in value than is truth, and philosophy is occupied with meaning." Not many of us are novelists or philosophers, but we find in informal ways that we ask the same questions.

You are promise. This can mean that your life has meaning, purpose and potential. But these qualities are not found through sudden conversions, at least not often. Admit the possibility that now and then someone in the dark is instantly enlightened. Recognize that some people are turned around from their course on a lonely road. These are rare instances. They do not often last. Most of us do not look for such occasions. Our sense of worth and promise is developed slowly and subtly.

For those who want to develop the sense of their own promise, I have tried to bring together some of the paths and turns others have taken that have proved worthwhile. No one should think of the following suggestions as ten easy lessons for people in pursuit of promise. Some of the suggestions may mean little to you; others may be just what you have needed. These are not assured counsels, but a description of actions and thoughts that have worked for other people.

**Try intervening
at the right moment**

This clue comes from the world of psychiatry or psychoanalysis. But it may be of value in self-therapy. Moving from promiselessness to promise is a kind of therapy.

The counselor may listen to the patient telling the story of his life. This could go on through countless sessions. "Yes, yes . . . go on. H-m-m-m. Is that what you mean? . . . Yes, yes." The therapist is nondirective. He has to allow time for some drift. The story has to come out first. The patient has to be able to set forth something with which to come to terms.

On the other hand, such telling could

Our sense of worth is developed slowly and subtly.

eventually become repetitious. It goes nowhere. Whitman would find animal sounds to be a symphony compared with such self-centered whining and weeping. You can so enjoy lying in bed in the morning regretting the day without promise. The siesta allows for noon's escape and the fiesta for evening's evasion. Regale your friends with the deep, deep thoughts that come to you in the waking hours of the night: I, only I, have ever been *this* aware.

Then, one day, you drop a hint to yourself. You have had enough of the wallowing. You are ready to take a turn. Here is where the act of intervening makes sense. A psychoanalyst, Herbert Fingarette, describes intervention. It is a suggestion to a patient that "a new conception of one's life may be worth trying, a new 'game' played."

At the appropriate moment of dramatic involvement a suggestion is offered, a new conception is possible *for you.* You can *experience* genuinely and *see* your life in terms of the meaning-scheme suggested by the words of the therapist. There may be a more unified life, there may be fewer meaningless gaps, if you follow the scheme.

Who knows when the appropriate moment comes? For some people, New Year's Day or a birthday is a symbolic occasion for making resolutions. "From now on, I'm going to try something different." Others latch on to an occasion—a contest or an opportunity appears. "I've had enough of staring inside myself and seeing no promise. I'll try anything."

The key word in Fingarette's rather difficult and compressed summary was "game." Life is here seen as a setting in which various games can be played by various rules. Promiselessness, in these terms, is a game. In it, one does not allow good signs to be recognized. Everything that happens can be ground down, worn down, thrown away, even if under normal circumstances it could have been promising. In the game of promise, a person permits a signal to be positive. Maybe something good can happen to open possibility.

No one can tell just what is the right moment, and in advance it is hard to say which new game will be appropriate. A new wardrobe might be attractive to a suburban matron, but I doubt if it would have a lasting effect. If she has been suffering from the disease of overconsuming, all she does then is continue consuming. More radical would be a career change. But career change can also be a running away. Still, these extremes and all the options in between have to be entertained. Anything that will interrupt drift and disrupt old patterns holds some promise.

"As if"
is a worthwhile game
This is a dangerous point, and I feel a bit halfhearted as I bring it up. A philosopher named Hans Vaihinger developed what he called an "as if" school of thought. Many people with less formidable names have stumbled on to the same idea. In this game or conception of life you try to change the future by treating something "as if" it were happening or were true. It may be. You do not know. You do not have eyes to see as yet.

"As if" is far different from the game of "let's pretend." "Let's pretend" begins with and remains content with illusions. It leads only to foolishness. The rabbi of Chelm is distracted by children as he prepares a sermon. He hollers out the window to chase them away: "Hurry down to the river, where a terrible monster is in the water. He is breathing fire and is an ugly dragon." The children run to see what is going on. People follow them. The crowd grows. As the rabbi sees the mob running he asks where everyone is going. "Down to the river, where there is a monster breathing fire; it's an ugly green dragon." The rabbi joins the race. "True, I did make it up," he thinks as he pants. "Still, you never can tell."

"Let's pretend" is pure fiction. "As if" represents an investment in the possibly plausible. You have not seen that you are promise; others see it. You act "as if," entertaining the game that they have found valid. You test it, and it may prove false. But there has at least been an occasion for change. You have not been merely skeptical or merely gullible.

When Theodore Roszak described *The Making of a Counter Culture*, he asked his readers to act "as if" the world were magical. At the time, his suggestion sounded foolish. He was talking to twentieth-century young people, inviting them to rebel against their fathers' world of machines. That world had too much rationality in it. If youth would act "as if" the world were magical, maybe adults would follow. The belief in technology would then be called into question. Society might make more intelligent use of its resources. People might find better terms for coming together, as the Indians had once done in their tribes.

The problem seemed to be this: the people to whom he was writing *knew* that the world was not magical. They had profited from the study of science. They knew about cause and effect. The human race had begun to get rid of ghosts and goblins after much effort. Why bring back the spooks and the spirits?

Maybe Roszak did have something, however. After all, he distinguished between kinds of magic. When he was finished, what he spoke for was not much different from what other people call a sense of wonder. And nature—in this queer universe—is wondrous. It has a magical dimension. Science, which sometimes works to dispel mystery, is also full of what looks like miracle. Acting as if nature were magical may really be attributing to nature the magic that properly belongs there.

Acting "as if" may be what Coleridge called a "willing suspension of disbelief." It will not produce belief. The false cannot become true as a result of the "as if" game. The game, instead, buys time. You have more opportunity to appraise something from many angles. "As if" helps you see what could have been overlooked had you not worn its spectacles. Acting as if the universe bears promise to you, or that you bring promise to it, would be foolish if there were no potential. But the potential may have been overlooked and this game permits you to start over again.

No one can really start over again. The record of broken pledges and unfulfilled promises piles up. But "as if" games permit or inspire the effort, and may be part of a pattern of self-fulfilling prophecy. To transform yourself means to recognize a different world to which you are present. The same old people will still be there, the furniture may remain the same, but the angle of vision changes. You remain condemned to meaning, but the choices are not as narrow. The stranger may become the one who unlocks something of the mystery about yourself. You may help the stranger. You will see something you had previously overlooked in the people close to you.

Many people have played the "as if" game and intervened on a pattern of drift in their lives. In the process, they changed their majors in college or switched jobs and found themselves. They decided to read a book and be open to it, and it changed them. Their drama starts over. F. Scott Fitzgerald's old saying that "there are no second acts in American lives" no longer need hold true. Those who play at "as if" encounter surprise, expect and find the unexpected.

The "as if" game will not always pay off. Some people use it to dream of Utopia.

Eventually, they find that the world does not offer them an easy living. But this approach does allow them to get inside a different scheme, to entertain a different view of the world, to try something on to see if it fits.

You will find it necessary to lose your illusions

It is a good idea to follow up the "as if" game with a reminder that the search for one's promise should not be based on false dreams. "As if" works only in a context of realism. If I am a balding, middle-aged professor with a slight build, I would be foolish to look for a new career as a halfback who moonlights as a matinee idol. (I don't think there are such people as matinee idols anymore; I use it only because it adds to the sense of illusion and madness, and it sounds good.)

The game of life deals many people a bad hand. If you are destined to spend your life in a wheelchair, to think of your promise as a ballet dancer is unrealistic. If you are president of the United States, you can tell everyone to be self-reliant. But simple self-reliance is a false dream for the people in the ghetto who need help. They (you?) would do better to play a game of life that teaches how to find help.

...the search for promise
should not be based on false dreams.

Illusions deny the tragic sense of life. People turn to the occult or to certain forms of religion to sustain illusions. They use symbols that relate to the future. No one can check these out. Someday, they say, our vision will prove to be true. Their lives are organized around that vision. Meanwhile, they make no contact with people in a loser's locker room, in a cancer ward, at a graveside, or from a loan company that is out to collect on bad debts.

Touch bottom early

The whole previous chapter was devoted to probing the breadth and depth of the problem of promiselessness. If one always tiptoes away from the sense of meaninglessness, sooner or later it will have to be faced. Sooner is better; from there one can begin to affirm again.

When an affirmative signal comes, affirm it

I have a friend who said that he found this exercise useful. Write on a card, "I hereby resign as boss of the universe." The resignation will be readily accepted. Then you are free for other things. Losing illusions and touching bottom prepare you for taking a modest place in a universe of meaning. Then, if something good happens, you can recognize it as good.

Many people have difficulty taking this turn. In a sense, it is more luxurious to remain pessimistic or totally apathetic. No matter what, you will not show interest. Saying yes involves a bit of a risk or a dare. Once this queer and unexpected universe gives an occasion for affirming, there is always the possibility that a second occasion may arise.

Negation can become comfortable. The child cries at grandmother's house as night falls in the guest bedroom. "But, child, you never cry when I baby-sit with you at home and you are alone in the dark." "That's different, grandmother. That's my *own* darkness." When light breaks in, even to dispel your own convenient and cozy darkness, you have to recognize it.

In the Middle Ages, people spoke of penitents as scrupulous. To be scrupulous meant to be so turned in on yourself that you could not notice outside signals. The scrupulous person went through the motions of seeking the grace of God, but in reality sought only to draw attention to himself. "How am I doing, God? Notice me, my brothers, I am more aware of my awful sins than anyone else." Such a sinner never looked up from the mirror long enough to recognize any stirrings of grace.

Dag Hammarskjöld, the late secretary-general of the United Nations, kept a spiritual diary in which he regularly addressed the question of saying yes.

In 1956 he wrote, "You dare your Yes—and experience a meaning. You repeat your Yes—and all things acquire a meaning. When everything has a meaning, how can you live anything but a *Yes?*"

Five years later, on Whitsunday, 1961, he enlarged on this idea. The passage also shows that Hammarskjöld could not really define the experience that changed his life; few people can.

I don't know Who—or what—put the question, I don't know when it was put. I don't even remember answering. But at some moment I did answer *Yes* to Someone—or Something—and from that hour I was certain that existence is meaningful and that, therefore, my life, in self-surrender, had a goal.

The mention of Hammarskjöld suggests something about the how of saying yes. When nothing else speaks to us, we can begin by paying attention to people who responded with a yes. I do not refer to superficial people, gullible converts to each

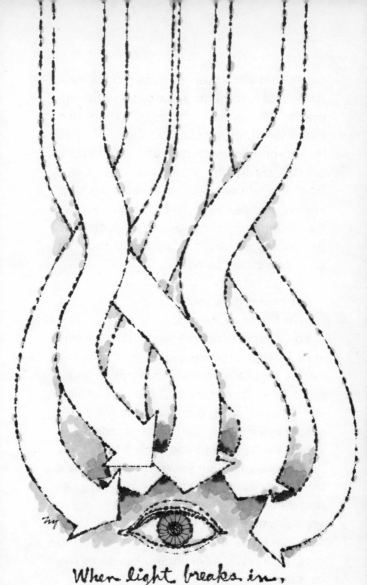

When light breaks in,
even to dispel your own
convenient and cozy darkness,
You have to recognize it.

cause that advertises itself, but to the cautious and profound individuals who appraise the signals carefully. When one hears yes from people who speak of good in the world only with difficulty, it acquires a special credibility. When strength comes from the wounded heart of man, we take special notice. Such great people are always indirectly available through the printed page, but it is better to look for someone closer to home.

Let yourself be found
by a friend or friends

You are promise, but you will not be very sure of that promise unless it is checked out by people who are important to you. I first wrote "find a friend," but that implies you should seek out someone who will satisfy your own particular needs. You would find it easy to use such a friend.

The idea of letting yourself be found by a friend has a different connotation. It implies that other people need you and may discern your promise. They will not be likely to do so unless you have given them reason to care, unless you have undertaken some risk as a friend to them.

It is difficult to write about being a friend to others without resorting to phrases that sound like nineteenth-century copybook

Let yourself be found
by a friend or friends.

maxims. Even the idea of encouraging friendship has an antique, pious ring. Maybe that in itself should alert us to the idea that friendship has been overlooked as a resource in recent times. The basic human needs behind having a friend or being a friend have not changed; the circumstances for becoming involved with others have.

For most people, the basic change in friendship patterns has come about as a result of the crowding together of people. The contrast between the old-fashioned village world of one-to-one relations and modern impersonality can be overdone. Maybe everyone knew everyone else in grandfather's village; yet friendship might have been rare. But getting to know others did not become easier when people began to live closer together in large, impersonal, and confusing cities.

A student of modern Berlin has said, "You can kill a man with an apartment just as you can kill him with an axe. It only takes a little longer." It is not rare for someone to live for years in a modern high-rise apartment six inches away from other lonely people on the other side of a paper-thin wall and not to meet them or to know more about them than their names.

For some time it was fashionable to say

that people who lived in apartments in big cities had chosen anonymity and had learned to relish it. From some points of view that is true. They do not wish to be butted in on. They do not welcome all the door-to-door salesmen and tract-passers who live in the city. They do not wish to share intimacies with all the people who pass by. The dangers of the modern city give them cause to withdraw.

Those who have experienced this mode of existence—and merely living in the city does not necessarily make one an expert on it as a way of life—report that the romantic notion that anonymity is okay has its limits. While residents often reject the world of gossip and trivial interference, they never quite learn to cope with the impersonality and loneliness. An acquaintance of mine once served as a minister in a modern urban apartment complex. From him I learned how hard it was to have a friend or be a friend there.

No medieval castle with a moat was more walled-in than were these buildings. High crime rates in the neighborhood made the residents feel besieged. Casual contacts were difficult and delicate. A visitor to the complex had to identify himself as he entered the parking lot or got out of a cab. A doorman stood guard over the main entrance. "Exactly whom do you want to see? I'll call her."

If "she" cooperated, the second hurdle was passed. Next came the unlocking of the passage to the elevators, another process calling for identification. Finally, the resident could refuse to open her door to you after looking you over through the peep-hole. On the way up or down on the elevator, you might talk with others about the weather or the speed of the lift, but in true ships-that-pass-in-the-night fashion, you and your fellow passengers would part at the thirty-eighth floor, never to see each other again. No risk of offering one's person to another could occur under these circumstances.

Do not picture our ministerial friend as a clerical-collared priest presiding at rites. Neither was he an unctuous minister in a shiny-lapelled suit cajoling kids to sing louder at Sunday School, or an organization man pushing ushers down an aisle with collection plates. He worked incognito at his honest worldly employment. His ministry was largely one of listening and of being available. He became well acquainted with coffee-shop waitresses and bartenders in the building complex. When they would hear the woes of a resident, they might pass on the word that there was a minister on the thirty-eighth floor. "Don't be afraid now, he's not what you'd think." He was a good listener and a friend. There were many barriers to be overcome before any significant exchange could be risked between him and his neighbors.

The high-rise complex is important because more and more people live in such an environment today and because it is symbolic of the growing anonymity in all aspects of our daily lives. The modern university campus does not differ much from the high-rise complex. Once upon a time, colleges were comprised of small groups of students who developed occasions for friendship in even more intimate subgroups called fraternities and sororities. Their activities may have been a bit frantic and contrived, but even their ritual helped reinforce a climate in which people could become important to each other and could check out friendships.

Today, the majority of collegians go to schools with ten to twenty thousand other students. More and more of these are community colleges. Some of them are called streetcar campuses because students travel long distances by public transportation to attend classes and then leave again. Except for classes and coffee breaks, there are few opportunities for students to meet one another. High schools bring people together a bit less formally for longer periods of time, but even high school students report that close personal contacts with other students are minimal.

The growing impersonality of our world has much to do with the concept of promise. Someone has said that a promise is binding in inverse proportion to the number of people to whom it is made. A politician blabs a promise to millions. No one expects it to be kept. But he promises himself to his wife; the odds increase—slightly, at least—that he will be more faithful to her. So it is also in the world of promise. People we are with day after day come to depend on us, trust us, and judge us differently than would the hundreds of people we pass on elevators or in corridors. The promise of your life binds you most to the small number of people to whom it is most visible.

The friend affirms the value of your life, even on those mornings when the day promises nothing. A friend may find a way to help you have the courage to face the 3 A.M. threat. Meanwhile, your friend looks to you for the same affirmation, and the expectation itself provides an opportunity for you to show your worth.

The French thinker Gabriel Marcel liked to talk about a quality called *disponibilité*.

Not quite translatable—if it were, I would not have used the rather forbidding French—it has to do with being open and available to someone else. You can see instantly how easy it would be to mess up the concept. Al Capp's *Li'l Abner* used to have a character called "Available Jones," who was available to perform any service—for a fee. He had no principles. Only a price. Being open and available could mean that a person is simply gullible, a doormat for all the world to tromp on. Or it could mean that a person is a meddler, snooping into everyone's affairs, ready to pounce on any personal shortcomings.

Disponibilité, however, implies that the available person has a core of worth or integrity. He gives of himself without becoming exhausted, because the giving adds to his inner treasure. What makes this person's availability valuable is that along with the inner core of integrity, there is a willingness to be vulnerable. People do not know each other's promise unless they become vulnerable to one another, unless they let down their guards. Letting down your guard is part of the risk of friendship.

Having and being a friend is not a formal counseling relationship; you have a friend for friendship's sake, not for therapy. Critics often wonder why United States presidents so frequently vacation with people who are not politicians. They often seem to have little in common with the chief executive. Some recent presidents have sought and enjoyed the company of comedians and clowns. A president has many political experts to counsel him during the long workdays and weeks. On weekends, he needs someone who is more important to him than a court jester to a king, someone who can put his routines into playful perspective and not take them all so seriously. His promise can better be checked out in his dealings with such a person than it can be in his workday dealings with impersonal officers of state.

As with presidents, so it is with other human beings. There are bosses, and there are employees who carry out the bosses' biddings. From these roles, people will seldom learn who they are as persons of promise. Modern society does not offer adequate substitutes for the older concepts of friendship.

Counsel is available, not always for a price

A counselor may be a friend, and a friend may be a counselor. But sometimes we need someone who can provide yet another view of our world. We began this discussion, for instance, with the idea that as we drift along in promiselessness, someone has to intervene at a strategic moment. But loved ones and friends often share in the drift and may not know when to interrupt or intervene.

A counselor has perspective that a peer does not. An old frontier story will illustrate the limits of what our equals can provide. A horse thief was arrested for stealing horses. Of course, he protested his innocence. Did he prefer a trial under a judge or by a jury of his peers? "What are peers?" "They are people just like you." "What, me be tried by a bunch of horse thieves?"

The president's clownish friend may be his fellow horse thief, just as our closest friends may be ours. The counselor may be a horse-thief peer to someone else, but he or she will have some experiences that differ from our own and can help us see in a special way. Counseling is, of course, a major and often expensive industry. It, too, includes contacts as impersonal as those one makes on an elevator ride. An example would be the advice columns in the daily newspapers. I would not dismiss them as useless. Sometimes they are written by gifted, witty people who, precisely because they cannot enter deeply into situations, can often humorously demonstrate the triviality of other people's problems and help us sort out our own true problems from the imagined ones.

Magazines, books, and pamphlets written by professionals in other fields can also be a source of counsel. Such experts may be successful as counselors, to the degree that they are open and vulnerable. Since they are professionals in a field other than counseling, it may be difficult for them to impart their sense of care to readers.

Actually, the test of our promise does not always come when we speak inside the safest zones of our expertise. We are tested by the degree to which whatever we say or do grows out of a single core of integrity. Take, for example, the various roles a modern Protestant minister may have to undertake when he talks about or offers love.

He may bounce his child on his knee and whisper words about loving the child. He uses different language with a different intent when he says, "I love you," to his wife. Then he gets up in the pulpit and says "beloved" to a mixed congregation. He has to have a different role or intention here, or he will be in trouble with many a husband or boyfriend. And if he writes an article on love for a church paper he may use even more abstract terms.

Such a person with so many roles may be phony in all of them. Some roles may come more naturally to him than others. People tend to trust him in some roles if they have seen him to be faithful and competent in others. I have often noticed how engrossed members of a congregation will be when they overhear an intellectual preacher talking simply to children. They make allowances for and even enjoy his simple language. They would not trust him so much had they not first heard him speaking on a more adult level. His promise was portrayed to them in part because he risked seeming childish to them, when he was only being childlike.

An athletic coach may play several roles. At game time, he will bawl out someone who has failed to execute a play, sometimes using language of scorn or, if the school board and parents are out of range, obscenity. You are nothing to him at the moment. As regrettable as some of that role-playing may be, you make allowances for it because in the course of three years you see it as part of human frailty. It is mixed with other roles in his general pattern of competence: he knows when humiliation will bring something out of you. And you have learned to confide in him in his office or in your locker room or in a stroll back from a defeat. There his care for you is based on risk, so you listen to his counsel.

The possibility of ministerial phoniness and the coach's lapse of temper or language serve as reminders that counselors are not perfect. Sometimes people choose them precisely because they can be fallible and mistaken. "If you can keep your head when all about you are losing theirs, you don't understand the problem." I have heard there is a toy that teaches adjustment to the modern world. No matter how you put it together, it does not come out right. The counselor has to know the confusion of situations, has to know about the many ways the world cannot be put together perfectly.

You will find yourself resisting some counselors simply because they seem so sure of themselves, so unwilling to say, "I don't know." You will be drawn to some who have had difficulty facing the promise of a day or a life. You realize that they, too, have been bored or terrified, have tried to evade questions and have come to realize their limits. A great philosopher of our century, José Ortega y Gasset, spoke of what we call promiselessness as the state of shipwreck. "The sense of being shipwrecked, since it is the truth about life, already means a measure of rescue. I therefore believe only in the thoughts of the shipwrecked." So do you, probably.

When we talk about vulnerable and fallible counselors, it is clear that one need not have a shingle above a door advertising expertise as a counselor. Now and then, highly qualified formal and professional counsel is necessary. The best advice that could be given then is "don't fool around." But, in many contexts, a sailor or a steamfitter may offer helpful counsel, if he is a thoughtful person. The counselor is someone who takes your promise seriously even when you do not. The weathering experience of the years is his great asset.

A larger framework for your life has to be found

That "shipwrecked" counselor is interesting to you because he or she has survived. They have found a lifeboat or an island shore, some place to stand again to view the world. The shipwrecked who remain at sea, clinging to a bit of wood, are not in much of a position to see your promise in perspective.

A partially fulfilled person stands within a framework or against a backdrop. Gordon Allport in his work *Becoming* tells us that coming of age implies "developing a view of a complete world." Such development may begin with an "as if" attitude, that "willing suspension of disbelief." A complete world does not mean that we have found the final secret of history and removed all mystery. It does mean that we will not be content with only "meaningless gaps," and will want to make whatever connections are possible.

Here we come close to circular reasoning. To know that you are promise you have to overcome meaninglessness. You overcome meaninglessness by finding meaning. When you find meaning you will have found promise. What help is all that? At this stage, our interest is not in suggesting a particular promise-filled meaning scheme. Later, a timid, half-shipwrecked statement of one option will be offered. For the moment, we can only urge that a search be undertaken. The friend or the counselor can help us relate the fragments of a haphazard life to a pattern of some sort.

Friedrich Nietzsche, the nineteenth-century philosopher who announced the death of God and whose larger framework was different from what I would seek or advocate, saw this principle clearly. "He who has a *why* to live for can bear almost any *how*." His contemporary, the Russian novelist Fëdor Dostoevsky, paralleled this:

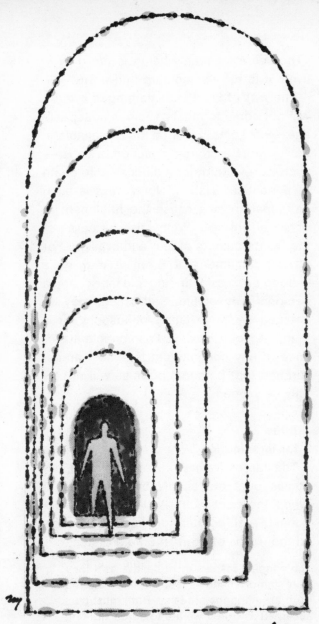

A larger framework for your life
has to be found.

"The secret of man's being is not only to live but to have something to live for."

The *why* of life, the something to live for, will not come to most people in neat packages. For some it will be most available in the form of a course of action, a cause— such as revolution or a defense unto death of a political system. Not always is such participation in a cause the fulfillment of personal promise. It may also be borne of the twin monsters of fear and evasion. For others, fulfillment of promise may be a lifelong process of finding and fabricating a personal way of life. Still others may be grasped by an existing philosophy or a religious point of view. Fashionable avoidance of any commitment is almost an assurance that personal promise will not be fully developed.

Allow
for imagination

The larger framework of fulfillment becomes ours not simply by grim pursuit. When the poet W. H. Auden won the National Medal for Literature in 1967, he quoted the words of novelist E. M. Forster.

The people I respect must behave as if they were immortal and as if society were eternal. Both assumptions are false. Both must be accepted as true if we are to go on working and eating and loving, and are able to keep open a few breathing-holes for the human spirit. . . .

Let's withhold comment about personal immortality; the fact that society is not eternal is obvious. In 2 billion years—if not sooner—that will have been proven to be true, as the earth freezes or fries. But we must live "as if" the larger framework will survive. And we thereby "keep open a few breathing-holes for the human spirit."

The fact that you are promise will not be visible unless you and those around you are successful in keeping open these breathing-holes. Society at large tends to do what it can to close them off. Elementary education was often a closing of breathing-holes. "Oh, Billy, *that's* not how to draw a house. Everyone else draws a house this way. . . ." "Mary, whatever got into you to call *that* poetry? Here is how everyone else makes a poem. . . ." The childhood world of wonder is thus suppressed.

In high school, in college, in unemployment lines, or in welfare lines, people are often treated like computer cards and feel that they have to live up to others' expectations. At work, the boss expects you to be imaginative—but not upsetting. When you would like to dance, the culture expects you to walk. When you survive spiritual shipwreck and want to report your experiences, you are a threat to others who are still at sea. A bit of light shines into your room, and others want you to shut it out; they are no longer afraid of their own darkness, and they do not welcome the dreadful freedom a bit of light might bring.

Resist them all, not because what you experience is right or logical for others, but because it is right for you. Resistance will not always be head-on and grim. Here the arts can offer support. The poet Edith Sitwell slightly overdramatized the case when she called for "the flower of magic, not of logic." I would not downgrade the value of logic and reason. But we have to recognize the degree to which the basic decision in life is related to juices and glands as well as to the intellect.

The dance, the arts, the imagination show the promise of a day from which we expected nothing. They provide breathing-holes for the human spirit in the midst of the noonday boredom, an alternative to frantic fiesta. They may not solve the problems that give rise to the 3 A.M. shock, but they address the question of limits that gave rise to that shock. Art and spontaneity mean letting things happen.

Here is where humor and play have their roles. Talking about humor and being hu-

Keep open a few breathing-holes
for the human spirit ...

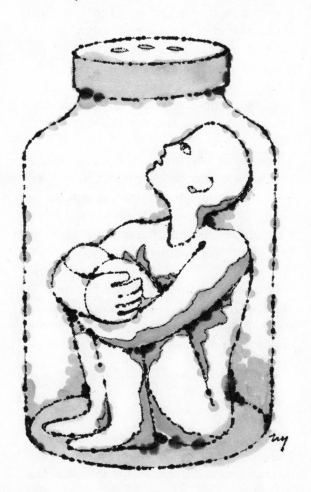

morous are two different things, but let us talk for a moment. Dour people are often put off by playful irreverence in sacred precincts. A modern scholar reminds us that there is a connection between the comic and the religious. "The inner essence of humor lies, no matter how heretical this may seem, in the strength of the religious disposition," writes a German scholar named Lersch; "for what humor does is to note how far all earthly and human things fall short of the measure of God."

The jester was needed to puncture the king's pretensions. We hope that at least one of the president's friends will be irreverent. The playful counselor will often do more for us than the sober-sided one. The adult world constantly pushes itself and youth too hard. In the realm of the spontaneous, human promise has its only chance. We cannot pierce the veil of existence, but we can create occasions where deeper stirrings can reach us. Imagination serves to do that.

Become active

I thought it would be safe to throw this one in right after talking about humor. It *is* a bit humorous for someone to announce that he wants to avoid copybook pieties and then turn around and talk like an old-time Scout leader. "Take a cold shower, boys. Up and at 'em. Be busy bees. The idle mind is the devil's workshop. Onward and upward."

At some point, we must move beyond the realm of "as if" in fulfilling the promise of our lives. Man does not live by bread alone, but he lives in part by bread. So we work and produce. *How* we do so is the important question. Becoming active is the first tentative step in trying out our promise in a new circumstance.

Becoming active does not mean joining an action cult. Scurrying around and being busy can be as evasive as Tennessee Williams's cocktail party. Revolutionary or reactionary causes can be made up of people with uncertain egos, reinforcing each other so that they never have to face the emptiness within themselves. Support of a religious movement can sometimes mean that a person has insulated himself from the kind of risks that gave birth to the movement.

Becoming active may mean testing one's promise. Vida Scudder, an early twentieth-century American liberal, lived ninety-three years. Asked how and why, she said that she had to jump out of bed every day to see

how the things she cared about and worked
for were turning out. She had proper credentials; she had not just been promising,
she had been giving. Becoming active
means that by our doing we seal the commitment made in words. "Promise her anything." Words are easy to waste. "Promises, promises!" But if we act, we build
and invest and test.

Becoming active means, then,
that promise is not related
wholly to the future.

There are those who think that
everything depends on their vision
and that someday
they will be proved right,
that everything will turn out
just as they have said it would.

Meanwhile, we must all press on,
press on.

I say you are promise,
and while promise hints at a future
and is open to it,
you do not have to wait
or to pursue the future only.
By present action,
you can begin fulfilling your promise.

When novelist Nikos Kazantzakis
said that because he did not hope,
he was free,
he underestimated the power of hope.
But he provided a good check
against those who say that promise
has to do wholly with a hidden future.

In our activity,
promise can begin to be ratified,
checked out, and affirmed
in the here and now.

four A model for our promise

When you are promise,
you act ''as if'' you are promise,
and you seek a larger framework
against which to test
the reality of your promise.

   Sooner or later the questions of meaning
versus futility become soul-size. They are
tested in the realm of the spirit. In the
Western world, the biblical tradition of
Judaism and Christianity has been a keeper
of the language of promise. Not for a moment am I ready to suggest that only people
who listen to the heritage have promise or
are promise. I do enthusiastically contend,
however, that resources in that lore are
often overlooked and deserve reconsidera-
tion.

A supermarket
of choices

The next time you scan the bookstalls at an airport newsstand, you will find that interest in the realm of soul and spirit has not declined in our time. Not long ago it was prophesied that people would either stop seeking meaning or at least lose interest in a religious framework or backdrop for their search. These prophets could not have been more wrong.

The covers on those books tell you that right in the midst of mysteries and science fiction, sports and suspense, there are hundreds of attempts to address the question of meaning. Then comes the second impression: by no means do all these speak along Judaic and Christian lines.

One of the strongest accents is astrological. The appeal of astrology is an obvious one, if a bit surprising in a world that was forgetting about signs and omens. Astrology argues that the movement of heavenly bodies affects your promise. You are important. You matter. *When* you were born separates you from most other people and in part predestines you to this or that course. You are promise.

Another section of books will be devoted to the occult and metaphysical. These words were not in common use many years ago. Today, people see in the occult and metaphysical a path to secret wisdom. Sometimes the teachings are similar to those of the ancient Persians or Egyptians. Maybe old gods of Greece and Rome are being revived in these books. Just as often philosophies not rooted in major historical traditions are presented here. In almost every case, there is a hint that secret sources of mysterious wisdom are available to initiates, which usually means, simply, to those who buy the book.

I never know how representative these books are of general and genuine concern about meaning. Of course, astrology has its devotees and serious students. Many of them have made it a lifelong interest and were not just recently attracted to it by its novelty. That some of the occult books touch on refined philosophies is also apparent. Ancient Gnosticism appears in modern dress. The world is viewed as a drama between two principles, one good and one evil. The line between substance and spirit is sharply drawn.

Just as often, though, these books have to do with nothing more than a passing fad. Someone is out for a fast buck. The authors may really believe what they are propagating, but their views on flying saucers, visitors from outer space, reincarnation, astral projection, and the like are so private and personal that they will disappear as soon as the books' first printings are exhausted. Their appeal is that they too say, "You are promise." It makes a difference how you live up to that promise, how you read the signs and wonders.

A third tier of books dealing with the spirit and soul may be approached more seriously. Many people of the Western world, weary of the search for meaning within the context of their own faiths, have turned to Eastern religions. Zen Buddhism is one of the most popular philosophies explored in these books, with yoga running a close second. The *I Ching*, or *Book of Changes*, and the writings of Confucius have their followers, while the wisdom of ancient Tibet is also represented. Some of the discussions are highly superficial, but publishers have also offered serious spokesmen of Eastern philosophy the opportunity to be heard, and they have found a hospitable audience.

Attitudes toward meaning and purpose are quite different in the East and West. The language of promise that we have been using links us with concepts of beginnings and ends, pasts and futures, goals and purposes. Few Eastern religions share this push-pull view of the universe. In fact, some of their appeal lies in the degree to which they help Western people keep from being overwhelmed by busyness and business.

Many of the Eastern religions offer people ways out of the salt mines, off the treadmill, away from the rat race and into Nirvana or some other spiritual state. Not in every case do these faiths promise that you are promise. However, I do believe that many people who buy these books as they dash to the next plane or the next sales convention use them as a means of learning their promise.

Words
from the West

Airport newsstands will normally stock only the more sensational Western religious works. Of course, the Bible will be there, and its whole message is not far from saying that a people and persons are promise. But the modern interpretations of the Judeo-Christian faith will usually accent the exotic and the dramatic. The humdrum aspects of synagogue and church life will be attacked or played down. After all, these authors are fighting off the noonday demon of boredom, which already makes regular appearances at eleven o'clock on a Sabbath.

Some of the Western religious literature is in narrative form. It will tell about people who have successfully brought the faith to those in the ghetto or in the drug culture. Maybe the story of a self-sacrificial physician's life will be featured. Authors will speak up for revivals and crowds in the "Jesus movement." They may emphasize the value of private prayer and devotion. Others will write about the future, especially about a prophesied end of the world. All of them will focus on some aspect of promise.

So biblical promise, as it appears on the newsstand, is a cafeteria line of options. A person may pick and choose, a dish of this and a dab of that, and pay at the end of the line. Many people are putting together their own views of the world in just this way. Margaret Mead, who is no conservative or hater of youth, has rued the fact that young people are making or having to make a mishmash of world religions because their parents did not successfully pass a tradition on to them.

Given this cafeteria-line approach, some people have felt compelled to advertise the superiority of their vision and then to argue about it. "My God is smarter than your God." "Mine delivers more." "Yours is false and mine is true." The question of truth-claims in religion is valid and urgent, but it is not likely to be settled in cafeteria-line arguments. In fact, it is not likely to be settled just because the question is now and then raised.

Overlooked
resources

What is more important than arguing old-style rationalist truth-claims is living with the faith's resources. People in the Western world who wish to examine their promise sooner or later will come across the biblical tradition. They are free to reject it or transform it, but they will find it difficult to avoid. The landscape and skyscape are dotted with towers of religious sanctuaries. The language and literature are full of traces of Judeo-Christian thought.

As far as living impact on the people is concerned, it is this tradition that says "You are promise" to most people. The pollsters may not tell us the whole story, but their evidence has to be weighed. Decade after decade, through religious revivals and depressions, returns and revolutions, the public remains constant.

About 70 percent feel that religion is "very important" to them, and 20 percent more find it "fairly important." Over 40 percent of them claim to have worshiped within the week. Eighty percent are "absolutely certain" there is a God, and another 10 percent are "fairly sure." Believe it or not, over 80 percent claim to believe in the Trinity—the Father, Son, and Holy Spirit. Over 70 percent believe that Jesus "was God." Almost 80 percent consider the Bible to be the revealed word of God.

The fact that about four fifths of the American people have some sense of being within the Judeo-Christian tradition has nothing to do with the question of its universal truth. Most people of the world do not share in this tradition. Many of our own exemplary local citizens are cool toward the tradition or turn their backs on it. Why then bring up the findings of the polls? They do not prove the truth, but they suggest the availability and pervasiveness of these beliefs. Any talk about meaning and promise in our culture must come to terms, pro or con, with biblical witness.

This witness is not only available, it is also influential. Judaic and Christian lore have influenced elements of our political life. For better or worse—and not a few say for worse—it provided us with views of nature that may have contributed to environmental pollution. While religious bloc voting is disappearing, this tradition helps shape people's views on some moral issues. In their private lives, they cling to it because it works for them. As John Dewey said, meaning has more value than truth in people's personal pursuits. So even those of us who cross our fingers, or are a bit lazy about thinking it all through, or "accept it all on faith" find ourselves temporarily setting aside some final questions about truth even as we relate to and possibly enjoy the biblical heritage of promise.

Judaic and Christian claims, then, have no monopoly in the world. And in many areas of living they do not even have reasons to seek a monopoly. Today, many of our religious representatives are open to the teachings of other religions and surrounding cultures. From them, they learn different ways of looking at time and history. You may be thought to be a crazy mixed-up kid if you spread yourself too thin in the cafeteria line of religion. You may become a taster of all and eater of none, a picky and choosy type. But fewer people than before will now discourage your spicing and seasoning your spiritual fare with elements all along the counter.

You will probably find yourself living your life between two extremes. On the one hand, you may affirm with Thomas Mann that the world has many centers, and that no single system will take all the weight of everyone's "as ifs" or "I believes." On the other hand, you will want to avoid becoming a kind of spiritual silly putty that absorbs all impressions and takes all shapes but is really nothing in itself.

Faith
creates problems

Since I am going to say something promising about the promise of biblical faith, it is only honest to preface my remarks with some reservations. Because the language of promise deals with the future, it can be dangerous. Some people read promise as dealing *only* with a life to come and become apathetic about the world around them. The Bible gives them no such latitude; it is constantly concerned with acting justly, loving mercifully, walking humbly with God.

The problem of the believer who drops out of the pursuit because of heavenly rewards in the hereafter is not as serious as that of the crusader. The crusader hears the word of promise, sees himself as an agent of fulfillment, and storms off to trample the temples of others. The fanatic must defeat the idols of everyone else and undercut their world views. He is licensed to disrupt all thought and life that does not agree with his own.

The Western, or biblical, traditions have

one other handicap. They are too familiar. For fourteen centuries Christianity was the official religion in all the West, and it still is here and there. (What self-styled believers did to the Jews most of that time is an unspeakable, but separate story.) After running the establishment, it became a part of the environment. As a result, it can be too familiar and boring.

We must face it. The same faith that wants us to realize our promise has often contributed to our sense of promiselessness. Countless people have awakened to a new day with nothing to look forward to because of a guilt imparted by a faith that wants to assure the removal of guilt. Other believers have faced the day without much sense of promise because "everything is in God's hands." They read the cards handed to them as if they came from a stacked deck.

The boredom and acedia of noonday sometimes look like a specifically Christian disease. Whoever has endured a long, droning sermon knows that faith may add to and not subtract from boredom, ennui, and the not-caring state. Because Christianity often condemned the fiesta, it drove people into subversive and guilty celebration. Incompetence among interpreters led many believers to misinterpret the anxiety that came to them in the twilight zone of half-sleep at 3 A.M. The religious record, in other words, is mixed. People will not instinctively turn to the tradition because of the institutions in which it is usually housed.

Being chosen

The basic claim of the biblical witness is that promise became part of history because of God's involvement with man. He creates; he cares; he in some way or other speaks to his people. The promise is focused when he chooses to speak to all people by choosing a people. The idea of chosenness helps you concentrate on promise; indeed, the languages of promise and chosenness are often connected in the Bible. Chosenness can also produce selfishness, fanaticism, and pride.

The Bible tells us that the Jews are God's chosen people. Through history, their chosenness has been a mixed blessing for them, a point that is humorously brought out in the story about a rabbi praying to God. The rabbi says that while he thanks God for the honor shown Israel when it was chosen, and while the treasure will be honored forever, "next time, if it is your will, could you see your way clear to choose someone else for this honor?"

The symbol of chosenness assured that the Bible would remain a book of promise. The promissory theme appears on almost every page. God himself can be seen as promise because he builds expectation about the future. Biblical faith is "infatuated with the possible," which is a good way of talking about promise. Time and space are taken seriously in biblical faith; a person does not try to escape them as in the East, but to be responsible within them.

The parable
of God

Christians believe that "Jesus, whom men call the Christ," the man of Nazareth, clarifies and embodies promise. For some, this means simply turning one's back on the Judaic witness—an attitude that the "book about Jesus," called the New Testament, will not permit his followers to hold. (See St. Paul's Letter to the Romans, chapters 9-11.) Others think that Jesus' "one way" means that they can learn nothing from and have nothing to do with people of other faiths, which is another idea that is qualified repeatedly in the New Testament.

Schubert Ogden links the promise in

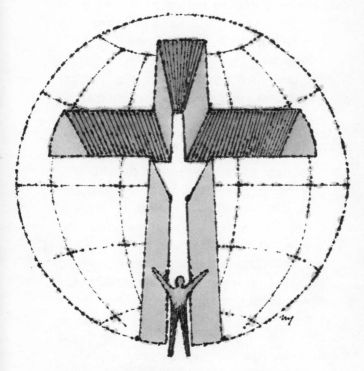

...promise became part of history
because of God's involvement
with man.

Jesus Christ with the whole world of promise. Divine love, he reminds us, is shown forth to people in every aspect of life. The believer stands by the claim that the decisive showing forth "is none other than the human word of Jesus of Nazareth."

Professor Ogden states, "The point of this claim is not that the Christ is manifest only in Jesus and nowhere else, but that the word addressed to men *everywhere,* in all the events of their lives, is none other than the word spoken in Jesus and in the preaching and sacraments of the church." One could come at it from the opposite direction: the promise spoken in Jesus is connected to "all things" in the world, and in him "all things" cohere, as Paul says in two of his letters. Not that there is nothing shocking or radical in Jesus' call to discipleship. But that scandal or shock to our system has to do chiefly with the ways in which we have to revise our pictures of God when we deal with Jesus.

Jesus cuts across the understandings of God that we normally hold. One student of Jesus' promise, Leander Keck, says, "He calls into question as a kind of 'parable of God,'" which does not explain God but points to him in a startling way. "Jesus not only tells shocking stories but leads a shocking life toward a shocking end."

This all connects with promise through the language of trust. Jesus "is affirmed to be trustworthy when those drawn into his orbit discover their deepest distrusts to be healed," and because in him they have the promise of a future.

Jesus was born, lived, and died a Jew. He lived in the language of promise in the Hebrew Scriptures. Today's Jew does not accept the "divinity" of Jesus, but he recognizes behind those claims a rabbi who talks of promise and turns people to trust in God. The Christian also trusts Jesus, which strikes some people as a strange idea, since Jesus "occurred" 2,000 years ago. Do we trust Caesar or Alexander? Why single out Jesus?

While some would say Jesus is the answer in the search for promise, I prefer to say that Jesus opens you to a better set of questions. You will be uneasy with previous solutions to the problem of life. You will be "in process," becoming a person of promise. Inside history, as Paul says, "you will know in part"; your knowledge will be piecework.

When we think deeply about the Gospel, we find that it is not simple to connect Jesus' promise to the world of our promise. Religious thinkers try. He provides access to all reality, says the believer. He is "the focus of being," who connects his followers to "a view of the world."

In some respects, Jesus is "just like one of us," but his believers step back when the questions get specific: "Like which one?" He is like us in that he is fully human, according to the New Testament "memory impressions" left by his followers. But as one thinker said, "he saved us by his difference from us." J. S. Whale helps us give words to our faith: "He is what God means by 'Man.' He is what man means by 'God.'"

The truth of these statements is not demonstrable in the laboratory or the logic class, though they may not be refuted there either. One can only ask people to "try on" these claims, in the language of "as if," and test them later in the realm of promise. The equally urgent question is, "How is his promise connected to ours; how is he made available to us?"

Jesus is an historical figure, just as are the Caesars. We do not relate to their promise. But we are called by the original witnesses to trust Jesus. Leander Keck, who has devoted much thought to the topic, once said, "One trusts a figure in the past when he trusts his integrity and the validity of what he stood for. That is, he risks making the trusted person a model for his own life. . . ." The trusted one becomes the war-

114

rant for our way of life and commitments, the lens through which we test our experience and questions. The difference between the believer and the nonbeliever has less to do with whether an event occurred—in this case, the life of Jesus Christ—than with how it is interpreted. Interpreting Jesus usually occurs through the prism of personal promise. We tend to decide about life in general when we are faced with his particular life: that is what is meant by a framework for our promise.

**The model
of promise**

I do not want to minimize the difficulties that go with any grasp of Jesus as a model for our promise. The documents about him were all written by believers. They see him from many points of view. Most of his world is inaccessible to us. Throughout history, believers have interpreted him in many different ways. Some have stressed that he was divine; others, that he was human. Recent people have made of him a poet of the Galilean hills, a zealot who wanted to revolt against Rome, a symbolic leader of black militants, a German intellectual, an East Harlem social worker.

Far from turning away from an interpretation of Jesus' promise because of these difficulties, however, we may use them to see in how many ways Jesus has touched the core of people's beings in many ages. While there may be a danger that Jesus simply be refashioned to suit everyone's purpose, those who are serious will find that the records of his life and word will also judge them. The varieties of response ought to keep everyone, at least, from claiming that they have captured and encapsulated Jesus.

He belongs to history; even faith in his risen life does not hide the fact that the record about him points to a different world than the one we inhabit. True, there are parallels in his life to the lives of people in what today we call the Third World, the counterculture, ghettos, revolutions and subversion, poverty programs, the affluent society, and the like. But essentially, his was a village and rural world, and only by strenuous efforts can his promise be linked to ours.

**Reading,
reflecting**

How does one go about it? One cannot avoid beginning with those memory impressions in the Gospel, set against the history of Judaism in the whole Bible. A few years ago, it would have been necessary for me to apologize at length for recommending that people would do well to read the Bible. Today, however, a new generation at least comprehends how and why it is that such texts have to be pored over.

Critic Leslie Fiedler observed that young people living in communes read in a different way than the detached scholars did. They might read the novels of Hermann Hesse or Ken Kesey, or they might probe *The Whole Earth Catalog.* In any case, they have read these "scripturally." That is, they have drawn the signals for their community from them. They ransacked and searched these sources and measured their way of life by what they read. Some of all that goes on in the reading of the Bible. No one has to care whether it is read from beginning to end. I doubt whether people get much out of that, with all the "begats" and repetitions. The Bible has to be plundered and searched for what has to do with one's promise. "Obedient listening to the strangeness of the Bible" provides its own shock to our preconceived notions.

Some people can get by with slogans. Back in the 1960s, radicals would often mouth a few formulas that they picked up from Chairman Mao or Professor Herbert Marcuse. But they did not penetrate the strangeness of these men's thought worlds and only used their writings. Biblical writings have been a source of culture, too. You can pick them up from posters and bumper stickers. But you will find that your priorities are rearranged when you let these writings reach you and upset you.

A second approach to the realization of your promise is that of reflection. Here, again, I would have blushed a few years ago to suggest that new generations might do well to collect their thoughts and meditate. The life of contemplation then belonged to Buddhist monks or Trappists in their monasteries. Not many years later a different attitude emerged. Collegians, dwellers in communes, surburban women at yoga classes, transcendental meditators, advocates of Zen—all were idling their engines and meditating.

Meditation in the biblical tradition is not an attempt to find a void, to remove oneself from history. It asks people to learn to be alone with themselves, to face the silence. Then they reflect on the promises of God, removing distractions from their minds. You might protest that such silent reflection has no place in a world of need. A lot of good it does to sit on your rump when you could be out world-beating, changing laws, or taking up collections for justice or for the hungry!

Meditating can be merely the latest diversion for the idle middle class, but it does not have to be. Thomas Merton entered a Trappist monastery to pursue the way of silence. With one side of his being, he followed that way. With another, he was a strong advocate for racial justice and peace—a true seer.

Henri Bergson, a philosopher of the early twentieth century, made a study of Christian meditators and mystics. He found to his surprise that they were people of great vitality and action and that "from their increased vitality there radiated an extraordinary energy, daring, power of conception and realization." The mystic's vision was "expressed in the bent for action, the faculty of adapting and readapting oneself to circumstances, in firmness combined with suppleness, in the prophetic discernment of what is possible and what is not, in the spirit of simplicity which triumphs over complications, in a word, supreme good sense."

I am not ready to defend the idea that this happened uniformly in the lives of all the mystics and meditators. But examples of such a combination come readily to mind, and can serve as a model. It does seem that most of the people who have breathed promise were people who could be alone

Meditation... asks people to be alone

with themselves—, to face the silence—.

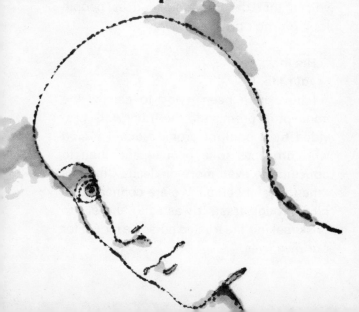

with themselves, in silence and solitude, before they reentered the world of action.

When we spoke about the Bible a little while ago, I did not mean to imply that you should be a "one-book" person. In the Jesus movement, particularly in some of its more temporary forms, it is fashionable to tell people to read only the Bible. Interpreters of only one book cannot be interpreters of any book. The Bible took shape in a complicated world; it spilled over into the world, and that world spilled into it. We read it in an ever more complex setting and develop understanding in relation to that complexity. The twenty centuries since the Bible was written have produced many voices that deserve a hearing as people look for their promise.

His life,
your life

I have here been trying to narrow the concept of promise to the framework provided by a book of promise about a God who promises to a people, and then to concentrate even more on Jesus Christ as "the focus of being." We are connected to him through trust, it was said, and are to "risk making the trusted person a model for our own lives."

Through all the confusing clues emerging from the sequence of Jesus' life, several promising leads for guiding our own lives develop. We need not make too much of the stories about Jesus' infancy, however attractive they may be during the Christmas season. They do suggest some of the weakness or helplessness of God, as Christians see it, when he brings his promise in this form. And the child is figuratively the image of opportunity, possibility, morning, springtime, having something to look forward to. All of life is promise. In these stories, Jesus is dependent and vulnerable. As a child, he does not offer us a framework.

Novelist Georges Bernanos points to the significance of Jesus' helplessness for the believer. "He did not come as a conqueror, but as one seeking shelter. He lives as a fugitive in me, under my protection, and I have to answer for him to the Father."

Of much more interest in modeling our own lives and sharpening our own sense of promise is the youthful aspect of his life and ministry. We are not here supporting a cult of youth. True, Jesus' enemies killed him by the time he was about thirty, so the now-aging "don't-trust-anyone-over-thirty" youth might find him a plausible, trustworthy figure. But we are not talking about biological states and chronological age. It is the openness and youthfulness of his ministry that impress us.

The Sermon on the Mount certainly breathes the spirit of a youthful adventurer. No church bureaucracy or committee would have come up with anything so promising or shocking. The way Jesus transcended the laws that he had come to fulfill when human need was involved still startles us. Life was promise for him even if he anticipated his eventual early death. There is a pace, a breathlessness about the narrative, even when it regularly tells us that Jesus withdrew and retreated to meditate.

The physicist John Platt says that Jesus did not even bother to give us a philosophy of life; he gave us a set of active verbs. They dealt with loving and healing, speaking truth and being ready to die. The way Jesus shattered the images to which men clung to keep themselves from seeing things as they were was youthful. David Roberts speaks for many: "There is something in all of us that cries out at times: 'What a relief it would be if I could just go ahead and live without having that Figure before my vision! Why can't he leave me alone?'"

Listen to this witness, Hans Urs von Balthasar: Jesus "is youthful by nature; he does not simply put one into an enthusiastic mood which will pass. He imparts substantially that Spirit which makes all things new. It is, inseparably, also the Spirit of Jesus who was always young." What keeps him young is the flaming word of God that "blazes in the Gospels and prevents the word of Christ from ever being completely at home in the disenchanted world of the grown-ups." This may be why the grown-ups who *really* catch his promise become creative misfits in their contemporaries' disenchanted world.

To follow him, then, is to "stand on the threshold of life where everything opens up, everything is promise. . . ."

What about the promise of Jesus' maturity? Today, maturity implies being resigned, compromising, disenchanted; those words will not apply to Jesus near his death. But he does address the world of adults. His awareness of impending death and his cry on the cross: "My God, My God, why hast thou forsaken me?" speaks to those whose hours are haunted by fear and evasion chasing each other's tail.

Jesus' ability to be spontaneous and to engage in creative schedule-breaking, as when he attended wedding feasts (which *then* went on for days), teaches adults how to measure what is important. But Jesus' attraction to adults does not mean that the figure of Jesus ever implies resignation, the dwindling of promise. Georges Bernanos shouted at his followers, "The gospel is eternally young, but you are so old. Even your old people are older than other old people."

The test of promise comes with Jesus' death. Death ends possibility and is the end of promise in the eyes of many. He did not welcome and did protest death, but did not seem to his followers at any time to picture this as the end of promise. These disciples, when they witnessed his "resurrection and new life," whatever else they meant by that mysterious witness, showed that for them his promise had not been exhausted by his death. The world had little room for the promise of justice and love that he embodied and inaugurated; the puzzle is how a disenchanted world could have tolerated him so long. In our time, the futurists in the Christian world like to say that, in this event, Jesus Christ "is still future to himself." The promise is not exhausted; the believer does not just look backward, is not a keeper of the City of the Dead, a custodian of an empty vault. The "not yet" marks trust in Jesus.

The disciples' memory impressions recorded in the Gospels and the interpretation of their meaning by Paul made clear that followers would be identified with him in his "death and rising." They see him inviting people to take up their crosses and follow him, not to kill the promise but to bring it to a new stage. All kinds of persecution complexes and death wishes have been clustered around this idea. We do well to remember that there is a difference between being "fools for Christ" and "damn fools." The tasks of embodying promise and discerning meaning suggest other ways of following him today.

Imitating, seeing

The idea of imitating Christ is an old and honored suggestion. Some great books and some poor ones have been written about it. The New Testament now and then makes room for it. But imitation has its limits, in part because the details of his life belong to the unrepeatable past. "What *would* Jesus do?" is not usually the best question to ask in today's world. The usual answer, by the way, is "he would do what I am about to do." This is all in the spirit of two men who argue and part with one saying, "All right, then, you do it your way, and I'll do it God's way."

Imitation can also be self-defeating, because the heroic way rarely fits into our ordinary lives, and we lose spirit. A student of Jesus' way, T. W. Manson, says something that may be of help: "The teaching of Jesus in the fullest and deepest sense is Jesus himself, and the best Christian living has always been in some sort of an imitation of Christ—not a slavish copying of his acts, but the working of his mind and spirit in new contexts of life and circumstances." Imitation in this sense means a rereading of the promise that you are in the light of Jesus' mind and spirit, as far as you can grasp from the Gospels.

Viewing my promise in the light of Jesus' promise occurs not just by imitation, then, but also by seeing him as a model for a whole way of life. The seeing is all-important. A scene in Carlos Castaneda's *A Separate Reality* shows in a vastly different context what vision can do.

"Once you learn, you can *see* every single thing in the world in a different way."
"Then, Don Juan, you don't see the world in the usual way any more."
"I see both ways. When I want to *look* at the world I see it the way you do. Then when I want to *see* it, I look at it the way I know and I perceive it in a different way."
"But . . . what's the advantage of learning to see?"
"You can tell things apart. You can see them for what they really are."

Is not this the vision implied in one of Paul's letters when he says that "if any one is in Christ there is a new world; the old order has already gone; the new order is already here"? "In Christ" is a formula that shows up in one form or other 164 times in the New Testament. It really means being found in relation to "his mind and spirit in new contexts of life and circumstances."

Seeing "the new world" is seeing the promise made new, having a fresh model. Here is the new birth of an "infatuation with the possible." The day begun "in Christ" is a day rich in potential surprise, for one "can see things for what they really are," and not in their dull appearances. The noonday devil does not disappear, but a resource for facing it is at hand. Festivity can be carried out in the spirit of the biblical wedding feast and not of the frantic cocktail party. The anxiety of nonbeing does not disappear. But by identification with Jesus Christ there is the possibility that his "new being" will shed light for us on darkness and terror.

No cure-alls are here. You still die.
You may get sick.
"You're fired!" is not removed
from the vocabulary of your boss.
Failure still haunts, and there are defeats.
But in no case

129

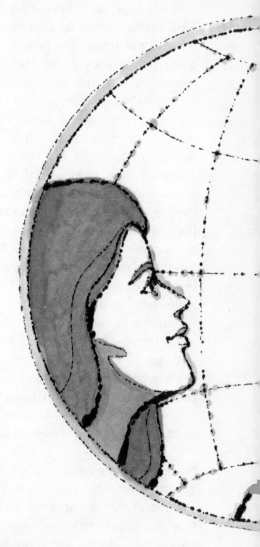

Here is a new birth of an

...nfatuation with the possible."

is the promise permanently denied
or forgotten.

The biblical word of promise
is like a pair of spectacles.
In Castaneda's "separate reality,"
you may still
"want to *look* at the world"
and see it as everyone naturally would.
Then it is all a threat to the promise.
But "when you want to *see* it,"
you look at it in a new way
and perceive it differently
to see things
for what they really are.

Somehow, they promise.

five **Relations**

Promises seek fulfillments.
You are promise,
and you will be fulfilled as you relate
to yourself, to others,
to the natural world, and to God.

At least those are the four directions
in which people have traditionally
tested their commitments.

The key word in all these relations
is care.

Care
of the self

Care of the self: excessive concern for
self can produce ego trips and dead ends.
People who concentrate on fulfilling themselves can be pretty dreary and boring, and
our society hardly needs more people who
are obsessed with themselves. On the other
hand, people are of little use to others, to
the world, or to God unless they come to
terms with themselves. You will recall that
we noted earlier how the language of false
humility can destroy images. "I am a worm,"
and who wants to be loved by a worm?

133

Most great systems of thought and many religions have tried to show how "man is the measure of all things." An old German Christmas hymn rejoices that God "honored our race thus, that he chose to dwell with us." Whatever else the model of Jesus Christ as a new human promise must mean, it can mean that people drawn to him acquire a new sense of the importance of being human. To speak further of the human as being unfinished or indeterminate, or to say that we do not yet know our outcome in an unexpected universe, is further to suggest the reasons for care of the self.

Such care does not have to begin by avoiding a tragic sense of human limits. Not everyone likes the old religious language about original sin. For them, it could be translated, "People are no damn good." When something has gone wrong with our promise and we take care of ourselves in isolation, we turn out to be damn worse. To get out of isolation is the goal of friendships, counselor relationships, quests for meaning schemes, or spiritual pursuits. The self "in relation" is capable of having realistic hope.

If you are a promise to be fulfilled, you will find that the attitude you take toward the future shapes most of your activities.

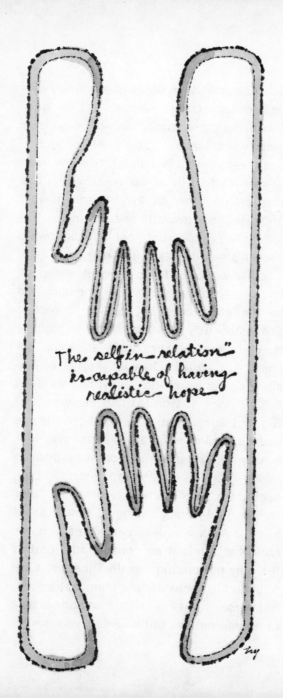

The self "in - relation" is capable of having realistic hope

Such an attitude is borne of extremely subtle decisions. Ortega reminds us that "decisive historical changes do not come from great wars, terrible cataclysms, or ingenious inventions; it is enough that the heart of man incline its sensitive crown to one side or the other of the horizon, toward optimism or toward pessimism. . . ." A self-hating generation gently tips toward pessimism and throws in the towel.

In the words of the old Scout leader, all you need is to pat yourself on the back and be "little engines that could." Jonathan Livingston Seagulls aspiring ever higher? Hardly. The realistic hope of which we speak has little to do with the life of illusions or the belief that everything will turn out all right. It won't. I like the words of Bernard Bosanquet: "Only that optimism is worth its salt which can go all the way with pessimism and arrive at a point beyond it."

Hope, far more than optimism, is connected with the promise of persons. Peter Berger, in *A Rumor of Angels,* remarks that hope is such a widespread element in our race that it might be considered a part of the human condition itself. Those who are reluctant to speak about human nature will, of course, not want to say that hope is part of human nature. But it certainly shows up as a virtually universal contributor to the human process and drama.

People hope even though they are aware of the prospect of death; they have seen others die and have mourned at gravesides. No thoughtful person can live with the illusion that death will not come to him or her. But somehow hope reappears, particularly among those who have learned that "love is stronger than death."

In the Christian world, hope is connected with the new life that is experienced in Jesus Christ. The New Testament says that his rising to new life represents the beginning of a "new creation," of which others are a part. This new life is also a present reality. In Christian history it is true that millions have lived chiefly with hope for an afterlife, but hope is not only to be connected with "deferred benefits" or "pie in the sky." The people of God in the Hebrew scriptures or Old Testament made very little of the idea of an afterlife, but they made very much of hope in a living God, who was working out his purposes in their midst.

In the modern world, hope is by no means only connected with hope for a second life. In fact, some enemies of the Christian version of the human drama—Karl Marx and most revolutionaries associated with him—believed that they had to dispel Christian hope in order to get people to invest in this life. The Christian record is a mixed one; sometimes people who hoped for a future life were passive and inert in this one. But just as frequently they have used it as an energizer for daily activity and change in the world. Be that as it may, alternatives to Christian approaches count heavily on the factor of hope. It is hope that one's cause will prevail or one's movement will matter that leads people to invest their lives.

While hope may be a virtually universal element in the human story, it can be suppressed and denied. As dangerous as living with illusions is the neglect of the hope factor. Historians commonly observe that people become active in the cause of improvement—whether of their circumstances or their world—only when a leader convinces them that they have some measure of hope for improvement. We hear people speak of "revolutions of rising expectations." When people are systematically beaten down and robbed of their humanity, they may very well simply accept their deprived status. Give them symbols of a cause and some reason for hope of at least partial success, and they will more likely rise.

In subtler and more intimate ways, we can see the principle of hope operate in the lives of ordinary people. Keep a young person bound in the hopelessness of a ghetto, and his potential will not emerge. Let him see an exit, a reason for living, a place where his talent can begin to develop, and he will more likely begin to fulfill his promise. In the Christian world, it is possible to use the language about God or Christ as a way to keep people down, to keep them waiting for a better round in the next life. But when people experience God as the power of the future and Jesus Christ—who lived without illusion, knowing the death he would face—as the intrusion of hope, they are enabled to blend realism about what they are with the promise of what they will be.

Healing
is waiting

The tipping of the sensitive crown of the human heart toward promise and hope is itself part of a cure. "Healing power is latent in men," writes David Roberts, "because it is latent 'in the nature of things.'" The universe can be viewed in two ways. It is cruel, marked by death, by the law of the jungle, by impersonal force. And it is marked by natural healing of wounds and the reaching out of loving persons. It is in the nature of things that others will be dependent upon you for reaching and healing. As you help fulfill what is latent in them you experience a measure of personal growth.

The genius and the misfit have taught us that people do not have to be bound by present horizons. We have already learned to come to terms with our genetic programming: not all of us have it in us to be opera stars or quarterbacks. We have turned in our cards as bosses of the universe and found the resignations accepted. We have decided that if we are not the Messiah, we should stop acting as if we were. But in that reduced orbit, the range of possibilities is still nearly infinite.

Self-hate, low self-esteem, and the notion that we make little difference in the world can be deeply ingrained. They become part of a personality, character flaws that cannot be wished away, removed by a few pep talks, or the reading of a 100-page book. One good bit of advice would be not to set impossible goals at the beginning of the cure, for disillusionment would soon set in. Some people keep a kind of spiritual diary, a sort of journal in which they record the tiny, tiny measures of progress in their effort to come to a better self-image. The

When we experience God
as the power of the future,
and Jesus Christ
as the intrusion of hope,
We are enabled to blend realism
about what we are,
with the promise
of what we will be.

more effective of these journals also balance the ledger with accounts of setbacks and a few entries of humbling humor.

At one level, however, there need be little narrowing of one's horizon or limiting of one's sights. If the goal of a person of promise is to see the world in a new way, to have a new style of consciousness, there seems to be no good reason for limiting in advance the boundaries. We have hinted that the human make-up may not actually change (short of the laboratory), but the self greets "an unexpected universe" in ways that allow for the development of new senses and sensibilities, new ways of seeing, new world views. In these terms, everyone can take part, from the Third World or the ghetto (where so much "consciousness-raising" is going on), to the world of bored suburbanites. Scientist Julian Huxley says, "Man is still very much an unfinished type, who clearly has actualized only a small fraction of his potentialities."

Resources are available on all hands for this opening of the person to promise. Some of them are overadvertised and full of perils; consciousness-expanding drugs are one of the high-risk shortcuts, a shortcut to nowhere as it usually turns out. To meet many tastes, however, a whole range of more modest but also more promising options beckon. Some of them may be fads in the hands of amateurs; the words mean many things to many people. But the encounter movement as a whole suggests opportunity. Forget the code words: sensitivity training, encounter groups, transactional analysis, therapy groups, intensive experiences. Behind them all is a recognition that we can change and be open to the promise of ourselves in relation to others.

**The gift
of affliction**

Unless you began this exploration a long time ago, it will surprise you to find how often growth occurs in the face of adversity. Many opportunities of the encounter industry are designed for reasonably affluent people living in suburban luxury. But whoever has lived with suffering or with a handicap knows that however discomforting these may be, they do not automatically rule out the possibility of new self-regard. For some time I have cherished a book by Melvin Schoonover, *The Gift of Affliction.* It takes the form of a number of letters written by a father who has transmitted a bone disease to his daughter. I would not trust the book if it were sentimental or sweet. Instead, it rages against God and the universe, against unheeding taxicab drivers

If the goal of a person of promise
is to see the world in a new way
to have a new style of consciousness

There seems to no good reason
for limiting in advance
the boundaries.

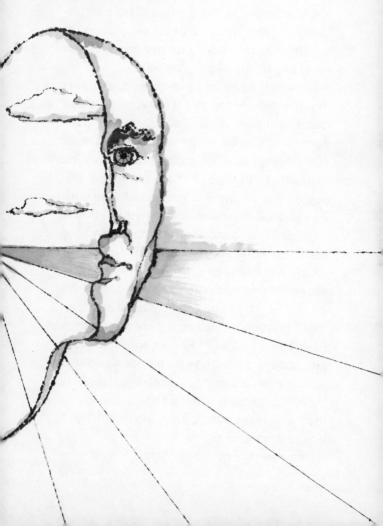

and militarists. Schoonover's occasional rages are borne of a sense of the self shaped by affliction, over which he has begun to triumph. Society taught him to hate his twisted body; he has found means to see his own integrity and the beauty of his existence. In the process, he has become of great worth to other people, and is a participant in more creative causes than most physically healthy people.

Care of the self involves finding, in nuturing, the core of the self. The word *core* can mean a basic, essential, enduring part, such as the heart (Latin: *cor*). You have an inner being, a depth that cannot easily be exhausted, though it can easily be obscured from view and neglected. The core can also be the center of something that is molded in a foundry. That mold can take many forms—delicate or solid, twisted or straight. It fulfills its purpose if the core was sound. "Does this person have a core?" we are asked. "Does he or she have a heart, an inner mystery or secret, a base from which risks can be taken?" People without a core are always and only to be found in the process of adapting, becoming relevant, trying to please, attempting to overcome their own insecurities. They are not of much use to others.

The self is not alone. Consciousness is

not changed in isolation. We are always "conscious of. . . ." We are conscious of that world that condemns us to meaning and in which promise must be found. So the self opens in relation to a second sphere, that of the world—and, specifically, the world of nature. Here is a second area in which care must be marked. Man may be the measure of all things, but he is not separate from all things. He is a late-appearing, half-welcome, spoiling stranger in the natural universe. He may not be around long. For a long time, he thought he could do anything he wanted to transform or to use nature. Suddenly, with desperate urgency, at least some of his kind have begun to recognize the precariousness of man's bond with nature. The ecological, environmental, and anti-pollution causes are public symbols of his awakening.

Care
of nature

Nature is promise. Just as we had to note that people are no damn good, so it is important that we do not sentimentalize nature. It exacts tolls in earthquakes and hurricanes, and the pleasant-sounding balance of nature is a relative harmony borne of pain and violence. But latent also in nature is stability, healing, and openness, and the human person has a chance to help bring out some of that potential.

The sphere in which nature most touches modern city-dwellers is that of sex. In fact, some scholars feel that modern obsession with the topic is borne of the fact that sexuality is one of the few areas of life in which people still meet the elemental, the earthy, the unpredictable. Most of the rest of the natural world is remote and inaccessible. Almost everything that is seen is man-made, packaged, controlled. But human sexuality allows for some free expression of spirit, unpredictability, caprice and creativity.

So sex is promise. It is promise as the genesis of generations, for producing new, unpredictable human beings. But in the normal course of things, its promise is revealed most frequently in the ways it deepens other human relations. For that reason, people who have the best interests of the race at heart would guard some of its mystery and prevent sex from being trivialized or rendered casual. Those who turn moralist take out the elements of play and humor or spontaneity, thus diminishing its promise.

Sex is not our sole contact with nature, however. In recent years, there has been considerable recovery of interest in the

nature is
promise

natural world on the part of our urban majority. Sometimes it shows up in quaint, almost pathetic, but still inspiring ways—in a flower planted in a tenement or high-rise window box or in hurried vacations to the mountain country, where Kodak-snapping tourists hop out of buses to take pictures because suddenly they see a sign, "Beautiful Scenery."

These superficial or limited approaches have been accompanied by serious efforts to live into nature's demands and harmonies. Back-packing campers, hikers, environmentalists, and poets are uniting to tell their contemporaries that Western man should not always try to dominate and thus limit the promise of nature. I like the phrase of John Tyndall, who spoke of "the promise and potency of all terrestrial life." Or the Protestant mystic Jakob Boehme; he spoke of "the torment of matter," its "drive, life, spirit, elasticity." Matter is motion, and the human who shares in its motion shares its promise along with its threat.

Care
of the other

The third sphere may be the most important: you see the promise of the "other," of other persons and of society. Care of the neighbor is one of the tests of your own promise. William James put it well: "Other people supply me with my existence." He might have added: and I supply them with theirs. Most of the forces of modern life work against the fulfillment of this promise. We are crowded together and do not know each other. Habit, custom, and taboo do not permit us to reach out and support the other. Only now and then are there the kind of interruptions that help us sustain promise.

I wrote earlier of Melvin Schoonover and his book *The Gift of Affliction*. He tells of an incident that illumines the ways in which people help fulfill each other's promise. He was an active protester against the Vietnamese war, and—relatively immobilized in his wheelchair—he suffered tear-gassing and other injuries to which the more mobile were less subject. He tells of a Washington march:

Over and over again we were warmly greeted; "How great of you to come," some said. Again and again we were offered food. I said to one young man, "Boy, a cup of hot coffee sure would taste good now." "I'm sorry I don't have any coffee," he replied, "but how about some Southern Comfort?" Another young man asked if I were warm enough and when I indicated that I really wasn't, he reached down and said, "Well, at least I can turn up your coat collar for you." And someone else gave me an impromptu back rub to help the circulation. And an obviously nearsighted young lady flung her arms around me, kissed me, and expostulated, "You're beautiful."

Schoonover is telling what others are doing for him; they could just as well report on what his presence did to open and sustain them.

Can a father look up from his newspaper long enough to listen to and really hear his son or daughter? Can a priest interrupt the institutional church's laws and routines enough to help someone whose problems do not fit in the usual slots? Do you really get by with a little help from your friends? Were the Indians better off when they lived in tribes than we are now, when we live apart from all others, except two or three family members, or live alone in dormitories or apartments? Can we experience again our part in a "people of promise," as sharers in movements, causes, group encounters? Can we be made aware of the degree to which well-meaning, if often mistaken, people invested in our promise, and of how much depends now on our investment in others? Are we able to sit through a long night of silence with someone who has known a loss and for whom words of chatter are less soothing than a personal presence would be? These are questions that cannot be answered in advance; motivations for answers will come from people who see themselves as being promise personified.

Tomorrow, promise may be discerned in areas where it was overlooked some decades ago, largely because people found each other. The movements of women's liberation, built on a sense of sisterhood, the forces of black power and dignity, based on a spirit of brotherhood—these are typical of the new agencies of promise in the world. Women's roles have begun to be more fulfilling; the white majorities are learning to see the blacks and other minorities as significant others with whom they have to reckon. Within the movements the major excitement has revolved around the discoveries we have made of the promise of people whose talents had gone unrecognized previously.

Care of the other means seeking his or her core as well as discerning one's own. The mystery of the personalities of other people is without bounds. I know an artist who can sit for hours in a coffee shop window simply observing people and seeing in virtually every one of them a subject for a drawing. He never tires of the infinite promise shown in the faces and strides of almost everyone he scrutinizes.

You also know people who have not yet learned how much others depend on them. It has been said that today grace will best be experienced through a gracious brother or a gracious other. Yet many people have heard words of grace spoken in the abstract, as in a church, but have never known tender regard or support from the people around them. Eventually, the words wear thin and are no longer believed. This concern takes us back into the orbit of Christian thought. Daniel Day Williams reminds us that "Christian maturity involves . . . progress in our capacity to love. . . . The difference between the beginning of life in love and whatever fuller realization of love comes to be may be slight indeed. . . . But there can be no Christian life at all unless there is some real meaning in progress in strength to express love."

Care of God

Little more need be said about the fourth zone, the promise of God. Today, there is much reappraisal of what people mean when they say "God." Many of them have learned that they should not say it lightly or cheaply, that they should be careful about its use. But if one trend seems consistent, it is to see God "becoming," God in motion toward man, God as promiser and as promise. According to the biblical story, he revealed himself to Moses in a burning bush. His words ("I am who I am.") can equally well be translated "I will be who I will be." He is recognized in the unfolding future.

This futurist picture of God does not mean that all old concepts have to be thrown away; they simply have to be seen in a new light. They do not mean that God is *only* future; "I'm damned tired of waiting," says a friend. But as the "God of promise," he is never exhausted by the words his believers invent about him. He opens new possibilities for himself and for them. The core of God cannot be known by man; on this the major faiths seem to agree. But if core also means heart, then Christians are ready to say that they have seen this heart in Jesus Christ, the parable of God, and in people who have been active in love.

Focusing on the promise of God is the only way a book such as this can keep free of illusion or superficial optimism. Insofar as affairs of self, nature, and others are within human control, there is little reason to affirm. The future of God and the promise of Jesus Christ do not make affirmation easy, and they do not make simple answers

155

available. They open the door for the yes that marks some lives, and they raise the level of questions. No books, prescriptions, or counsels have done away with cancer wards, concentration camps, refugees, racial prejudice, poverty, and natural terror or death. But the gift of promise makes it possible for people to meet life on the terms that existence hands them. Very often it is the very witness of people in the concentration camps or refugee centers, the afflicted victims of cancer, and those who have known suffering who most cherish promise.

So it is with aging. Much of what I have written seems designed for the twenty-year-old for whom life is opening. I would like to think that it applies as well to the seventy-year-old, even if age has sharply restricted some options of life. True, the aged person has to be more aware of limits than before, but the contexts will still remain large. As one of the world's oldest people told Dr. Alexander Leaf, "every day is a gift when you are over 100." (Or, as the blind man of 123 said, when asked about his relations with women, "I can't see them too well anymore, but by feeling, I can tell if they are women or not. Oh, to be 108 again!")

Maybe nothing more happens in retirement communities than the attempt, as one

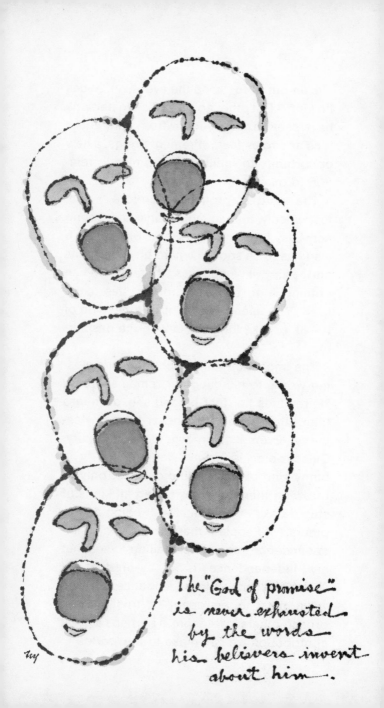

The "God of promise"
is never exhausted
by the words
his believers invent
about him.

citizen put it, to "keep the ever-livin' juices flowing." But other aging and aged persons have seen in the freedom from care about jobs and roles that retirement brings, a new opportunity to fulfill their promise in relation to others.

The word of promise, therefore, is *not* tested only among collegians and young activists, honeymooners and prodigies. It also has to be spoken where physical limits and pain or loneliness threaten. When nothing is to be said, promise has to be lived. You spend the night at a bedside of the ill, or take long walks with the despairing.

The impact of Melvin Schoonover's closing words to his daughter remains strong. He reminds her that he and she, even less than other people, can never have any security. Even illusion would be a luxury. Catastrophe is always imminent. "In a funny kind of way we find our lives only by throwing them away, by taking all kinds of stupid risks" to physical well-being and to others. "People marvel at my 'independence,' completely failing to see that my independence is a by-product of acknowledged interdependence. . . . The willingness to be open, to trust, to approach others in freedom is perhaps a great contribution we can make to the world."

Transfusions
of grace

Father and daughter depend, then, upon "transfusions of grace" that help them know victory beyond evil and suffering and death. Schoonover's book cannot close on a "down," nor can this one. It seemed important to recall that affirmation of promise sometimes occurs more readily among the afflicted, the aged, or the handicapped than among the thoughtlessly healthy.

What people are learning
is to appreciate the intrinsic worth
of themselves
and of others,
the promise of a world
and of a God of promise.
Such a vision
will keep them from letting victories
lead to pride,
or letting defeats lead to despair.

We have gone full circle.
Here is where we came in,
with a hypothesis
that can be tested
in life's circumstances:

You are promise.

Selected references

Allport, Gordon W. *Becoming* (New Haven: Yale University Press, 1955).

Balthasar, Hans Urs von. *A Theological Anthropology* (New York: Sheed and Ward, 1967). See section on "The Word as Youth," pp. 258 ff.

Berg, R. H. quoted in Elton B. McNeil, ed. *Being Human: The Psychological Experience* (New York: Canfield Press, 1973), p. 71.

Berger, Peter. *A Rumor of Angels* (Garden City, New York: Doubleday, 1969), pp. 75 ff.

Bernanos, Georges. *Diary of a Country Priest* (New York: Macmillan, 1937), p. 189. Also quoted in Balthasar (see above).

Boehme, Jakob, quoted in Gajo Petrovic. *Marx in the Mid-Twentieth Century* (Garden City, New York: Doubleday, 1967), p. 189.

Camus, Albert, quoted in Huston Smith (see below), p. 24.

Castaneda, Carlos. *A Separate Reality* (New York: Simon and Schuster, 1971).

Dewey, John, quoted in Huston Smith (see below).

Dostoevsky, Fëdor, quoted in Huston Smith (see below), p. 39.

Elmen, Paul. *The Restoration of Meaning to Contemporary Life* (Garden City, New York: Doubleday, 1958), chapter 2.

Fingarette, Herbert. *The Self in Transformation* (New York: Basic Books, 1963), p. 25.

Haldane, J. B. S., quoted in Loren Eiseley. *The Unexpected Universe* (New York: Harcourt, Brace and World, 1969).

Hammarskjöld, Dag, quoted in Henry P. van Dusen. *Dag Hammarskjöld: The Statesman and His Faith* (New York: Harper and Row, 1967), pp. 100 ff.

Keck, Leander E. *A Future for the Historical Jesus* (New York: Abingdon, 1971), chapter 5.

Leaf, Alexander. "Every Day is a Gift When You Are Over 100." *National Geographic,* January 1973.

Lersch, P., quoted in Hugo Rahner. *Man at Play* (New York: Herder and Herder, 1967), p. 35.

Nietzsche, Friedrich, quoted in Huston Smith (see below), p. 39.

Ogden, Schubert M. *The Reality of God and Other Essays* (New York: Harper and Row, 1966).

Ortega y Gasset, José, quoted in Karl J. Weintraub. *Visions of Culture* (Chicago: University of Chicago, 1966), chapter 6.

Price, Roger, and Stern, Leonard. *What Not To Name the Baby* (Los Angeles: Price/Stern/Sloan Publishers, 1972).

Rilke, Rainer Maria von, quoted in Sebastian de Grazia. *The Political Community: A Study of Anomie* (Chicago: University of Chicago, 1948), p. 11.

Roberts, David E., quoted in Edmund Fuller, ed. *Affirmations of God and Man* (New York: Association Press, 1967), p. 32. See also David E. Roberts. *Psychotherapy and a Christian View of Man* (New York: Charles Scribner's Sons, 1950), chapter 9.

Roszak, Theodore. *The Making of a Counter Culture* (Garden City, New York: Doubleday, 1969), chapter 8.

Schoonover, Melvin. *Letters to Polly on the Gift of Affliction* (Grand Rapids, Michigan: William B. Eerdmans, 1971), pp. 91 ff.